Chanukah Tu b'Shvat Tu b'Av & Purim

Matityahu Glazerson

Published by Kings Judaica, 2023.

While every precaution has been taken in the preparation of this book, the publisher assumes no responsibility for errors or omissions, or for damages resulting from the use of the information contained herein.

CHANUKAH TU B'SHVAT TU B'AV & PURIM

First edition. December 17, 2023.

Copyright © 2023 Matityahu Glazerson.

ISBN: 979-8224461646

Written by Matityahu Glazerson.

CHANUKAH

*

TU B'SHVAT

*

TU B'AV

*

PURIM

CONTENTS

Introduction

MATITYAHU GLAZERSON

The Holy Tongue & Gematria

ON THE UNIQUE STATUS OF HEBREW, THE HOLY TONGUE

From *Pardes Rimonim*, *Sha'ar Ha-Otiot*, Chapter 1:

Many have supposed that the letters of the Hebrew alphabet are a matter of symbolic convention, that the Sages decided and agreed among themselves that certain signs would represent the sounds of speech. For example, they agreed that the sounds made by closing the lips would be represented by the forms of the letters: *beit* (ב), *vav* (ו), *mem* (מ), and *peh* (פ) - and likewise for the remaining sounds of the language. In the same way, other peoples also have symbolic representations for the sounds of their languages.

According to this view, there is no difference between the Hebrew letters and the alphabets of other nations. The Hebrew letters are the conventional symbols used by the Israelite nation on the advice of Moshe through his prophetic inspiration, and the other alphabets are the conventional symbols of the other nations.

It follows, according to this theory, that the written words are nothing more than a means for making known the intent of the speaker. For example, a doctor who writes a book about healing art doesn't intend that the book itself will be medicine; rather, he intends that the book should make known his thoughts or preferences on the subject of healing. Once the reader understands the principles of the healing art as written in the book, the book itself is of no intrinsic importance. Thus, if a person studies the book for years on end but does not succeed in learning the principles set forth therein, his study has done nothing for him and his soul has not been improved at all, since he still does not understand the requirements of the art. In fact, his study has actually done him harm, since he has wasted time and effort without gaining understanding.

The Torah, according to those who hold this view, is just like the medical textbook of our example; its purpose is to reveal the inner meanings and processes necessary for the perfection of the soul and if one does not master the required knowledge, he gains no benefit from his studies (God forbid).

This theory, however, cannot be true, for undoubtedly the words of Torah **"restore the soul"** (*Tehillim* 19:8). The proof is that the *Halachah* obligates us to read the weekly Torah portion, twice in the original Hebrew and once in the Aramaic translation, and this includes even seemingly meaningless place names such as *Atarot* and *Divon* (Bemidbar 32:3). This teaches us the perfection of the Torah: the very words and letters themselves have hidden inner mean-ing, spiritual power, and vitality.

From Chapter 2:

The letters of the Torah are not simply written according to the agreed convention. Indeed, their form reflects the inner essence of their soul, for the shapes of these letters - the tiny extensions at their tips (*kotzim*), their "crowns" (*tagim*) and their component elements (*tziyunim*) - indicate definite spiritual concepts and supernal *sefirot*. The spiritual concept of each and every letter contains a glorious light, derived from the essence of the *sefirot*, which devolves [to this world] by stages, in accordance with the developmental order of the *sefirot*. Each letter is like a splendid palace, containing and corresponding to its spiritual concept.

When one of the letters is pronounced aloud, the corresponding spiritual force is necessarily evoked. Speaking Hebrew assumes holy forms which rise up and are sanctified at their root, which is the root of [the highest Kabbalistic world, known as] *Atzilut* (אצילות, "emanation"). These spiritual forces here not only in [the vocalized letters] but also in their written forms...

From the Words of Rabbi *Tzadok* Ha-Kohen in his work, *Or Zarua* La *Tzaddik*:

The Kabbalists, of blessed memory, the Sages of the Truth, taught that all the supernal worlds were created by combinations of the holy letters. And in this [lower] world, every created thing is kept alive by virtue of its name in the Holy Tongue. Therefore, the name which [Adam] gave to each thing (see *Bereshit* 2:19) is its true name. For example, the essential life source of the שׁוֹר (*shor*, "ox") is the force of the three letters שׁ, ו, and ר, in the upper worlds. It is the same for all earthly creatures and likewise for the created beings of all the worlds. Thus, every perceptive person will realize that it is fitting and excellent to call this language the "Holy Tongue" for it is truly holy.

<u>GUIDELINES TO GEMATRIA</u>

To aid the reader in understanding the basic concepts of gematria employed in this book, some of the essential principles are summarized here.

1. Primary gematria: counting the numerical value of each letter

The thirty-two principles of exegesis used by the Sages to interpret the Torah are set forth in a *barayta* in the name of Rabbi Eliezer the son of Rabbi *Yosei Ha-Gelili*. The twenty-ninth principle is primary gematria. The commentary Mid-rash *Tannaim* states that the numerical values of the Hebrew letters were given to Israel at Mount Sinai. The values are as follows:

1 — א	10 — י	100 — ק
2 — ב	20 — כ	200 — ר
3 — ג	30 — ל	300 — ש
4 — ד	40 — מ	400 — ת
5 — ה	50 — נ	500 — ך
6 — ו	60 — ס	600 — ם
7 — ז	70 — ע	700 — ן
8 — ח	80 — פ	800 — ף
9 — ט	90 — צ	900 — ץ

The last five letters listed here (corresponding to the numbers 500-900) are the "final" forms of the letters כ, פ, צ, נ, and מ, used when the letter comes at the end of a word. Sometimes these letters are assigned the same value as the regular form; for example, ך is counted as 20, just as is כ. But sometimes the "final" forms are used, as shown above, to represent the multiples of one hundred, from 500 through 900.

2. Reduced gematria (*gematria ketanah*) or small numerical value (*mispar katan*)

The *mispar katan* is the primary gematria (see previous section) with any final zeroes removed. Thus, both 10 and 100 are counted as 1.

This type of gematria is basic to the teaching of *Tikkunei Zohar*, one of the basic works of Kabbalah. It is connected with what the Kabbalistic writings refer to as Olam *Ha-Asiyah*, the World of Action. This, the lowest of the worlds, is symbolized by the units, while the tens and hundreds symbolize the higher worlds. (See *Ramchal, Adir Ba-Marom*, P. 65.) Thus, when we reduce a word to its *mispar katan*, we discover how the concept represented by that word relates to *Olam Ha-Asiyah*.

Sometimes the primary gematria or the *mispar katan* is reduced even further by adding together all the digits of the number. For example, we saw above that the gematria of פרנסה is 395. This can ultimately be reduced to 8.

$$3+9+5 = 17$$
$$1+7 = 8$$

3. Full gematria: writing out the name of each letter

In this form of gematria, each letter of a word is written out in full, and the numerical value of all the resulting letters is counted. For example, by the full gematria, the value of קו is 696.

4. Interchangeability of letters which are formed in the same part of the mouth

Sefer Ha-Yetzirah, an ancient Kabbalistic work, states that the letters may be divided into five groups, based on the part of the mouth where the letter is produced.

1. **אחה״ע**. These are the guttural letters, formed in the throat, using the back of the tongue and/or the pharynx.
2. **בומ״פ**. These are the labial letters, formed primarily by closing the lips.
3. **גכ״ק**. These are the palatal letters, formed mainly by contact between the palate and the back third of the tongue.
4. **דטלנ״ת**. These letters are produced with the tip of the tongue against the front of the palate just behind the teeth.
5. **זסשר״ץ**. These are the sibilants, produced by expelling air between the teeth with the tongue held flat.

5. The Atbash (את בש) transformation.

According to *Midrash Tannaim*, this type of equivalence was also given with the Torah on Mount Sinai. Therefore examples of it are found in the Talmud and Midrash. In the *Atbash* transformation, the first letter of the alphabet is interchangeable with the last, the second with the next-to-last,

and so on. This results in the following table of equivalences.

ע	–	ז	ק	–	ד	ת	–	א
ס	–	ח	צ	–	ה	ש	–	ב
נ	–	ט	פ	–	ו	ר	–	ג
			ל	–	כ	מ	–	י

6. The Albam (אל בם) transformation

This type of equivalence was also given with the Torah at Mount Sinai, according to Midrash *Tannaim*. According to this transformation, the letters of the alphabet are divided into two groups. The first letter of the first group is interchangeable with the first letter of the second group and so on.

א – ל	ה – ע	ט – ר
ב – מ	ו – פ	י – שׁ
ג – נ	ז – צ	כ – ת
ד – ס	ח – ק	

7. The Ayak-Bachar (איק בכר) transformation

According to the *Midrash Tannaim* the twenty-seven letters of the Hebrew alphabet are divided into three groups whereby each of the letters in the same group has the same small gematria. (The final letters are included in this transformation.)

א – י – ק	ד – מ – ת	ז – ע – ן
ב – כ – ר	ה – נ – ך	ח – פ – ף
ג – ל – שׁ	ו – ס – ם	ט – צ – ץ

8. The addition of the *kollel*

Sometimes, in finding the gematria of a word, we increase the total by one. Rabbi Y. A. Chaver, in *Pitchei She'arim* (p. 252) explains that in such cases the root (*shoresh*) of a word is still attached to the upper world.

An example is the word ברית (*brit*, "covenant"*). Its numerical equivalent, including the *kollel*, is 613.

ברית: $2+200+10+400 = 612$

plus the *kollel*: $612+1 = 613$

There are a total of 613 Scriptural *mitzvot*. Therefore we can say that this gematria teaches us that the concept of *brit* is attached and cleaves to the 613 *mitzvot*.

A related practice in gematria is to find the total numerical value of a word and then add the number of letters of the word. By this method, the word דגל (*degel*, "flag") has the numerical value of 40.

דגל: $4+3+30 = 37$

plus the number of letters: $3+37 = 40$

The Ba'al Ha-Turim finds a Scriptural basis for the practice of adding the kollel to a gematria. In the verse,

"Efrayim and Menashe will be the same as Reuven and Shimon" (*Bereshit* 48:5), the words, "Efrayim, Menashe" have the numerical value of 726, while "Shimon, Reuven" have the numerical value of 725. Thus, when we add the *kollel* to the second pair of words, the values are equal. And the Torah itself testifies that they are "the same." This is a hint that sometimes it is necessary to add the *kollel*.

אפרים מנשה:

$1+80+200+10+40,+40+50+300+5 = 726$

ראובן שמעון:

$200+1+6+2+50,+300+40+70+6+50= 725$

plus the kollel: $725+1 = 726$

Rabbi Ya'akov Emden, in his commentary on *Pirkei Avot* entitled *Lechem Shamayim* sets forth (at the end of Chapter 3) basic principles for the use of gematria.

One cannot use gematria to introduce into the Torah innovations which are not confirmed by our early forefathers, who had direct and trustworthy traditions. However, one may use gematria to uphold the teachings of our Sages and the traditions of our forefathers, and whoever originates such gematria - his reward will be great. For this purpose, the scholar is allowed to search tirelessly for a gematria with which to support the words of truth.

It is in this spirit that the author of the current work has not only cited many instances of gematria and related exegeses from other authorities but has also included some that do not appear elsewhere.

The Letters of the Alphabet as a Key to Understanding the Torah

Why is the Torah written without any indication of the beginning and the end of each verse, or of the proper vocalization of the words, i.e., without punctuation or vowels?

Rabbenu Bachyei answers this question in *Chovot Ha-Levavot*. He says that this is in order to enable us to discover numerous and varied new meanings by punctuating and vocalizing the Torah in ways other than the standard ones, and by grouping the letters into new words, different from those which appear in our Torah scrolls. In this way, hidden worlds are opened and revealed to us. For example, Ramban writes in his commentary on the Torah that in the first words of the Torah: בראשית ברא, ("In the beginning [God] created"), the letters can be divided in a different way to read: בראש יתברר ("It was created with [or for] the head").

This can add a new dimension to the understanding of the verse. An entire book has been written about all the possible combinations of the first word of the Torah, בראשית.

In this same light, the *Gaon* of Vilna explains the Gemara passage' dealing with the last eight verses of the Torah, in which the death of Moshe *Rabbenu* is described. The Gemara asks: How could Moshe *Rabbenu* have recorded his own death, which had not yet occurred? One of the answers suggested is that the Holy One, Blessed is He, dictated these verses to Moshe, "and Moshe wrote them with דמע (*dema*)." One possible meaning of the word דמע is "tears"; however, the Gaon says that this is not the correct interpretation. Rather, the meaning is "a mixture," as in the expression *terumah medama'at* (תרומה מדמעת), meaning sanctified food which has been "mixed" with ordinary food. That is to say, Moshe wrote the words describing his own death, but with the letters and words "mixed." Only after Moshe's death did Yehoshua discover that these letters, ordered differently, described the passing of Moshe.

This same idea can explain why the angels pressed their claim to *Hashem* that the Torah should be given to them rather than to the Jewish people. At first glance, it would seem that the angels' claim is incomprehensible since the laws of the Torah are relevant only to people of flesh and blood and not to Heavenly beings.

The answer, as the Sages tell us, is that *Hashem* already had the Torah with Him, in the form of all of its letters, before He created the world. But the letters were combined into words only afterward, forming the Torah as we k.10w it. (This is similar to the process by which Yehoshua, after the event, reconstructed the verses describing Moshe's death.) The angels wanted the Torah to be given to them but with the letters combined into words appropriate to their Heavenly nature.

The Hebrew letters help us to understand the Torah in other ways, too. In the introduction to his commentary on the Torah, Ramban lists the ways in which Moshe *Rabbenu* received the Torah from the mouth of the Almighty. These include (1) the simple meaning, (2) hints and allusions, (3) the numerical values of letters and words, and (4) teachings derived from the shapes of the letters, as well as other, similar methods. The *Tanna* Rabbi Eliezer, the son of Rabbi Yosei *Ha-Gelili*, lists thirty-two hermeneutic principles by which the Torah is expounded These include gematria (the numerical analysis of letters and words) and acrostics (join-ing the initials of words to form new words).

Let us consider, for example, the word לב (lev, "heart"), whose gematria is 32. Just as the heart is the source of life for the body, the thirty-two hermeneutic principles of Rabbi Eliezer are the heart of the Torah and through them, we can receive the life that the Torah gives. The letters of לב are the first and last letters of the Torah: *Bereshit* begins with ב, and *Devarim* ends with ל. The letter ל represents למוד (*limmud*, "study"), as we shall see below. The letter ב represents "inner" meaning - its name is *beit* (בית, "house," "interior") which is found in the Torah in the expression "*within* the curtain" (מבית לפרוכת).

Ba'al Ha-Turim notes that these two letters, ב and ל, are the only two in the alphabet that can be combined with all the letters of *Hashem's* name, י-ה-ו-ה, to make meaningful words: בי (*bi*, "*in me*"), בה (*bah*, "in her"), בו (*bo*, "in him"); לי (*li*, "to me"), לה (*lah*, "to her"), לו (*lo*, "to him"). None of the other letters have this feature: the letter מ, for example, can form meaningful words when combined with the letters י and ה, but not with ו. The significance of this observation is as follows: The heart (לב) is the point through which one can become completely connected to his Creator (י-ה-ו-ה). To this end, one must strive to make his heart pure and devoted to *Hashem*, thus achieving perfect attachment to Him.

The *Zohar* tells us that the Jewish people, the Torah, and the Holy One, Blessed is He, are One. Through the thirty-two (לב) hermeneutic principles, one becomes connected to the Torah, which is made up entirely of names of the Holy One, Blessed is He. The fact that the Torah is enclosed, as it were, by the letters of the word לב (*lev*, "heart") suggests to us that Torah study depends upon the heart of man, and also upon the thirty-two (לב) principles of interpretation. Why are these two letters found in reverse order, i.e. the ב at the beginning of the Torah and the ל at the end? This is to teach us that only through reviewing his studies, i.e. "going back" over them, can a person connect his heart to the Torah and come to know it through the thirty-two hermeneutic principles.

When read in reverse order, the word לב becomes בל (*bal*, "not"), indicating negation. One's life depends upon the heart; if one uses his heart properly, it can bring him to perfection. Otherwise, God forbid, it can bring him a feeling of lack and negation. *Kohelet* says: "The heart of the wise man is to the right, and the heart of the fool is to the left."

That is, when we read the word from the right, לב (*lev*, "heart"), it shows the way of the wise; from the left, בל (*bal*, "not"), it shows the way of the fool:

CHANUKAH

THE FESTIVAL OF CHANUKAH

Meaning of the name Kislev

Before learning about the many ideas of the festival of **Chanukah**, it is worthwhile understanding what is behind the meaning of the name of the month in which **Chanukah** falls, - כסלו **Kislev**. We find written in our holy books, that the root of the name of the month – - כסלו **Kislev** denotes - כסל fortitude and **security**, as we find written in the scriptures, the word -**Kislev** - כסלו applying to **Confidence**, "Whose confidence shall be cut off." ((כסלו) "אשר יקוט כסלו" –Job, <u>8:14</u>). The name Kislev teaches us about this month, in which the **security** and **confidence** of **Israel** was shown to the world, with the story of **Chanukah.**

A deeper explanation of the word **Kislev** is found by splitting the word - כסלו-**Kislev** into two words, כס- **Kas** (covering), לו, The Numerical value of לו-, equals 36, (6=ו 30=ל), referring to the **hidden/covered light**, which was shining for **Adam** for **thirty-six** hours in the days of Creation, and the **Thirty-six** candles that we light during the festival of **Chanukah**, are corresponding to them.

Another explanation for the name of the Month **Kislev** - כסלו is indicated in the letters of the word כסל-ו- כסלו. As mentioned before, the word כסל means **security**, so כסל–ו, means, **the security of the letter, "ו".** The letter "I", in Kabbala, represents holiness and truth. The letter "ו" is related to **Joseph,** who is connected to the **Sixth sphere,—** יסוד . **"Foundation"**. **Six** is the numerical value of the letter "ו".

As it is known, the Greeks intended to defile and contaminate purity from Israel, by defiling the oil in the Temple and contaminating the **Jewish** girls. So, the war was against **Joseph**, whose essence was Purity, and this is why he was called **Joseph the** - יוסף הצדיק

Righteous. The connection of **Joseph** to the Six Sphere is indicated in the numerical value of 80=ף 60=ס 6=ו 10=י) **Joseph** - יוסף together =156) which is **Six times** the name of **GOD** 10+5+6+5) **26** - (י-ה-ו-ה 26)x6=156). Interestingly, those who were against the Holiness of **Joseph** had the same numerical value as **Antiochus** –אנטיוכס 1+50+9+10+6+20+60) together=156) and also the same numerical value as) מלך יון King of Greece) (50= ן 6=ו 10=י 20=ך 30=ל 40=מ together = 156).

The interesting phenomenon in gematria is that the opposite powers have the same numerical value, which is based on the idea of the creation, that **GOD** created the world in such a way. a famous example of it is the words – משיחMessiah, and **Snake** - נחש which is a symbol of the evil powers – משיח((358=50+8+300-נחשMessiah – (40+300+10+8=358) shares the same numerical value.

Another interesting connection between **Joseph** and **Chanukah** is found in the dream of **Pharaoh**, The king of Egypt. The dream which Joseph interpreted to him. In his dream Pharaoh Saw, **"Seven ears of grain, solid and healthy, grew in one stalk"**, indicating to the **Menorah** in the **Temple**, which had seven lamps. According to the Kabbala, the Chanukah Menora is the extension and continuation of the Menorah in the Temple.

Another connection between the dream of **Pharaoh** to **Chanukah** is found in the verse, **"out of the Nile there came up seven cows, handsome and sturdy"**, and then, in the continuation of the dream, **'"seven other cows came up from the Nile close behind them, ugly and gaunt"**, and afterward, the ugly gaunt cows ate up the seven handsome sturdy cows"** indicating to the few **Hasmoneans** who consumed the wisdom of the **Greeks**, and then used it for the Torah. This fits with what we mentioned before, that the wisdom of Greece entered into the wisdom of the Torah,

That wisdom of Greece is indicated according to Zera Kodesh in the inner letters of the numerical value of the full letters of **Greece** יון –

ו)-נו (ו)-א-ו (ד)-יו (73=56+7+10),) which equals **Seventy-three**, which is the same numerical value of the word **"חכמה"** – **wisdom**, showing that **יון** - **Greece**, had wisdom, that with the victory of the Hasmonian, entered to **ציון**Zion, source of Torah.

The beauty of the Greece language came to them from the blessing to **Yefet**, " **"יפת אלה-ים ליפת וישכן באהלי שם"**The beauty of Japheth **shall be in the tents of Shem,**", The beauty of, **Greece - יון** is indicated in the letters of the word **יון** - **Greece**, which have the same letters as in the word **"נוי"**, meaning **beauty.**

Another connection to **Chanukah** is found in the portion of - **Miketz - מקץ**, the word, **"מקץ"**, which means in Hebrew, **in the End.** According to the Medrash and the Zohar, indicates to the verse in Job,(28:3) **"קץ שם לחשך"**, **'"He put an end to Darkness"** .

As we saw before, the Medrash says, that **Darkness** is the kingdom of Greece, which wanted to darken the eyes of the Jewish people from seeing the light of the **Torah.**

Another connection of **Joseph** to **Chanukah** is based on the Medrash which compares **Israel** to **oil,** –**שמן** in Hebrew. Comparing Israel to **oil** shows that **Israel** is like **oil** which does not mix with other liquids, Israel does not marry other nations.

Israel comparison to oil is indicated in the full numerical value of the letters of the word **שמן** –oil. The full gematria of the letters of the word **שין מם נון** –**שמן** equal 546 – (360+80+106=546), which is the same gematria as the name **Israel- "ישראל"** with the five letters, (10 +300+200+1+39+5=546).

When we take the inner letters of the full name **Israel– ישראל** the letters which are, , **מ-ון** –**יין**the number which comes out of it is **Joseph** - 60+40+56 =156), **יוסף**), showing the righteousness of **Joseph** in Egypt. that like oil, separated himself from the Egyptians, and did not marry a non-Jew.

It is interesting to note, that the story of the dream of Pharaoh, appears in the Torah, in the Portion of **Miketz - מקץ**, in the book of

Genesis (chapter 41) which most of the time, is read on the **Sabbath of Chanukah**.

THE SECRET OF THE NUMBER THIRTY-SIX

There is more depth to the number **Thirty-Six** than what is seen on the surface. Numbers **3** and **6**appear after the numbers **2** and **5**. **2** and **5** together create the number **25,** which is the date that the festival of**Chanukah** begins.

The commentary, Rokeach, fascinatingly points out that there are **thirty**-six mentions in the **Torah**, of words that are connected with the idea of light, for example, **fire, lamp**, etc.

Throughout **Chanukah**, there are **thirty-six** candles lit in total. According to the Jerusalem Talmud, (Berachot, chapter, 8, 8), the reason for this is to signify the **hidden light** which shone upon Adam for **thirty-six** hours, on the sixth day of creation. Each night that we kindle the Chanukah menorah, we are in fact drawing light from this **hidden light.**

The number **thirty-six** is also the number of tractates in the Babylon Talmud, also known as, The **Oral Torah**. The **Oral Torah** beginning started with laws initiated in **Chanukah**. This establishment occurred after the **Hasmonean** victory over the **Greeks.**, the Rabbi's brought a proof from the Torah, that **the Torah can be translated to the Greek language, from the verse** the Torah, "יפת אלה-ים ליפת וישכון באהלי" "May God enlarge·*enlarge* "Japheth, And let him dwell in the tents of Shem"(Genesis,9,27).

Yefet, the son Noah, is the forefather of **Greek civilization**. Within the wisdom of Greece, were tools and keys which were specified to adorn the wisdom of the Torah. **Shem**, the son Noah, is the forefather of **Jewish civilization.**

THE ORAL TORAH AND CHANUKAH

Rabbi Tzadok Hakohen says that the time that The **Oral Law** developed to its full potential came out after the victory of the **Hasmoneans**, over the **Greeks.** This culture of Greece .in a Jewish form, entered into **Judaism**, known in **Kabbalah** Characterizing and deep analysis of the Greek's virtues, was converted to Jewish values, with the victory of Israel over the Greece. The spiritual powers of **Greece** are revealed in the significance of the letters, of the name **Yavan.** Containing the Hebrew letters, **yud, vav ,nun - י ו ן** , the same letters as in the name **Ziin - ציון**, **yud vav,nun,** with the addition letter,**Zadi, -צ**in its beginning, representing the character of righteousness in Hebrew.

THE NAME ZION AND CHANUKAH

This idea is indicated in the word **Zion -ציון**, which is the place in **Jerusalem** about which is written in the verse (Isaiah 2, 3) **כי מציון** " "תורה" **תצא**From **Zion Torah will come out,**", **Zion** is a distinguished place in the studying of the **Torah.**

This is the Torah which controls and contains the element of the Greek culture converted, as it is indicated in the three letters of the name **Greek, Yavan, yud, vav, nun,** the same letters in **Zion,** as we saw before.. The letter **ו, ,ו,Vav** represents mystically, truth, and sanctity, in **Judaism**, which came out on **Chanukah,** with the victory of the **Hasmoneans.**

In the Month of **Kislev,** the element of Judaism, **sanctity, and holiness**, was secured. It is interesting to note that the candle represents the letter **ו, Vav,** in its shape. The number **thirty-six,** is also the number of the hidden righteous people. The **thirty-six** hours, the time that the **hidden light** in the time of creation was lightening to Adam, from the creation of Adam, until the end of Sabbath, when the darkness of the night came. The result of the sin of Adam. The number thirty-six is also the total number of the tractates in the **Babylonian Talmud.** This fits with the idea, brought in Kabala, that the hidden light is concealed in the Torah. This idea is hinted in the Hebrew name **Masechet-מסכת**, tractate, which in Hebrew is connected with the word **,Masach-מסך** which is from the word **veil**, and **cover**, indicating that the tractates of the **oral law**, acts as a veil for the hidden light. The Light which God purposely concealed within the Torah for the righteous people. This light was given as a means to pierce the darkness of the Greek exile. Thanks to the righteous **Hasmoneans,** this light came back in the light **of thirty-six candles of Chanukah.**

THE HIDDEN LIGHT AND CHANUKAH

Every year, the **hidden light** is revealed during the eight days of Chanukah. The light of the **Oral law**, which grew stronger and stronger after Israel's triumph over the **Greeks**. This light had previously been obscured by the darkness of Greek rule over Israel.

The righteous **Hasmonean, Matityahu** , and his sons, through their unbounded dedication, liberated this light. The number **thirty-six**, kabbalistically, represents the completion of the sphere of **Yesod - foundation**, the **sixth sphere** which represents Righteousness, which is the sphere of **Josef** the righteous. This idea is indicated in the numerical value of the of name **Joseph**, 156=10+6+60+80) יוסף) whose gematria is hundred and **fifty-six**, which is the gematria of **six** times the name of **G-od**, **twenty-six**,(26x6=156), the same gematria as the word156=)90+10+6+50 ציון,) - **Zion**. Both names represent similar idea, **sanctity,** and **holiness.**

The date of **Chanukah**, the **twenty-fifth** of **Kislev**, is exactly three months after the creation of the world, which was on the **twenty-fifth** of the month **Elull**. Three months after, the time of creation indicates that **Chanukah** is a kind of dedication of the world, as the meaning of the word, **Chanukah,** besides the original meaning of **Chanukah**, the dedication of the altar which was defiled by the **Greeks.**

The holiday of **Chanukah** as the epitome of the righteousness of Israel, finds expression in the Numerical value of the word —חנוכה**Chanukah**, which is **ninety,** with the total, (8+50+6+20+5+1=90) for the word. The number **ninety** is also the numerical value of the **letter**צדי - **tzadi**, the letter which represents righteousness. **Josef**, whose outstanding virtues, as we will see later, is connected with **Chanukah**.

THE FESTIVAL OF CHANUKAH

AND SUKKOT

The **Sefas Emeth** says, that against each of the three festivals of the Torah, **Passover, Shavuoth, and Sukkoth**, will be established in the future, by the Rabbis, in the time of the exile of Jews, **three festivals**, which will bring the light of the festivals of the Torah, into the darkness of the exile.

Two of those festivals were already established, they are **Chanukah**, which has eight days, which are against the eight days of the festival of **Sukkoth**. The festival of **Purim**, which is one day, is against the festival of **Shavuoth**, which is one day.

On **Shavuot** the Jews accepted willingly only the written **Torah** the written Torah, but the oral Torah, they did not want to accept, and GOD gave them by force.

On **Purim**, when the Jews saw the greatness of the righteous, **Mordechai,** and **Ester**, they accepted the oral Torah willingly. So, the festival of **Purim** competes with the festival of **Shavuoth**, completing this acceptance of the **Oral Torah,** which was given in Sinai on the Festival of **Shavuoth.** A Festival of seven days, in the future, which is against the festival of the Torah, **Passover,**

will be established in the time of the **Messiah**, on the time of the final Redemption.

THE CONNECTION OF CHANUKAH AND SUKKOTH

The Rokeach (Rabbi Eliezer Garmazia) on the verses in the Torah dealing with the commandant of lighting the lamps of the **Menorah**, in the holy Tabernacle, those verses appear in the Torah, after the laws of **Sukkoth**.

The commandment of the **Menorah** in the Tabernacle, says the Rokeach, on the verses about the lights of the **Menorah** with pure olive oil, for the light, the torah starts in singular, to lit the light, and afterwards in plural **" to arrange the lights",** this supports the ruling of **Beit Hillel**, who say that one should start lightening the **Menorah** of **Chanukah**, with one light, and then, increasing the lights.

This idea is opposed to that of **Beit Shamai**, who says that one should start with eight lights, and decrease the number of the lights every night.

The connection of **Sukkoth** and **Chanukah** is in their main principles, which are **Faith**, and **Confidence** in **GOD**.

The connection of **Chanukah** and **Sukkoth** is recognizable also from the similar idea which these three new festivals represent, On **Chanukah**; the central theme is the victory over Israel's enemies, and the revelation of the divine Presence. Similarly, on **Succoth,** the sacrificing of the **seventy oxen**, represents the hostile nation of the world, symbolizes the destruction of Israel's enemies. The main figure **of Chanukah** and **Succoth is Aaron**, the high priest. The medrash says, that **Aaron** was very sad because he did not participate in the dedication of the Tabernacle, God consoled him by giving him a function in the Tabernacle, Greater that these of the princes of the tribes who brought sacrifices at the dedication.

The Ramb**an** cites the medrash, stating that the consoling to Aaron was the eternal lightning, which is the kindling of the **Chanukah** lights, which will continue even after the destruction of the Temples. for this we are, indebted to Aaron.

CHANUKAH AND AARON THE HIGH PRIEST

Tikuney Zohar also comments that **Chanukah** expresses the grandeur of the attribute of **Aaron**.

An interesting connection **between Chanukah** and **Sukkoth** is brought about by the midrash, the Greeks who did not allow Jews to keep the festival of **Succoth**, strengthen this faith, which came out in a festival of eight days, the festival of Chanukah which was established for eight days.

As the festival of **Sukkoth** is based on **faith** in God, so the festival of **Chanukah** against the days like **Sukkoth** was established, a Festival that in its center, is faith and **confidence** in God, which is **Chanukah.**

Chanukah as a symbol of the defence and security of **GOD** on the children of Israel, is seen in their journeys in the desert, which are mentioned in the book **Numbers**, in the portion Massaei. Those **forty-eight journeys** in the desert, according to commentators indicate to the journeys of Jews in the future.

The **twenty-fifth** station, (the date of **Chanukah**, the **twenty-fifth** of **Kislev**) name of was **Hashmona**, a name connected with the heroes of **Chanukah.**

THE MEANING OF THE NAME CHANUKAH

The name **Chanukah** contains two words, **Chanu—Kh**כה - חנו - - Encamped in the **twenty-fifth which** is the date of **Chanukah.** According to **Kabala**, it indicates to the Divine glory which was on the children of Israel in the exile of **Greece**, in **Chanukah.**

The same happens in the **Sukkah** in the festival of **Succoth**, the Glory of GOD dwells in the **Sukkah.**

This connection of **Sukkoth** and **Chanukah** is seen from the same gematria of the two names which are the names of **God**) 65-**אדנ-י**), the name which represents **Judgment**, and the name, represents **Mercy** 26=10+5+6+5)) (26)**י-ה-ו-ה**) both name (65+26=91) **ninety-one, The splitting name of כה חנו חנוכה,** as **we saw before,,** with the two words (64 +25+2=91) like the word **סוכה** - **Sukkah** (60+6+20+5 =91).

The number **ninety-one** is the numerical value of the root of the word **Emuna, Amen**- 91=1+40+50))**אמן**In **Chanukah** and **Sukkoth**, **Faith**, and **Confidence**. are the basis of them. The main goal of these two festivals is to instill in the hearts of the people, **belief** and, **faith** in **GO, Faith** and **Belief**, that these festivals represent.

There is a special Prayer, added to the prayer of the Amida, on **Chanukkah**, which starts with the words **in the days** "**בימי מתתיהו**"- "of "Matityahu. This part contains **ninety-one** words.

ANOTHER EXPLANATION FOR THE NAME CHANUKAH

MAnother explanation for the name - חנוכה-Chanukah, according to our sages, is the construction of the holy **Tabernacle,** which was ready, on the **twenty-fifth** of **Kislev, God** however, delayed the dedication until the month of **Nissan,** the month of our father **Isaac.**

Even though the **twenty-fifth of Kislev** did not realize for the dedication of the **tabernacle**, it was nevertheless appointed for the rededication of the second **Temple,** when the **Hasmoneans** purified and deconsecrated it's after which the **Greeks** had defiled with all the vessels. The connection of **Chanukah** and **Sukkoth** which complement each other, is seen from the numerical value of חנוכה 1+89+486=570) פורים) **and the** spheres **foundation** and **kingdom-** 576=80+496) יסוד –מלכות. Another connection of **Sukkoth** and **Chanukah** says the Chidushei Harim (Chanukah)It is its connection with the laws of the Bikurim, the first fruits that have to be brought to the temple in **Jerusalem.** It Is on the festival of **Shavuoth,**

but if one did not bring it then, he can bring it until **Sukkoth,** and if he did not bring it then, he can bring it until **Chanukah.**

CHANUKAH AND THE NAME OF GOD

As it is known the four letters of **GOD** name,, י-ה-ו-ה are again the spheres, the letter - בינה - ,understanding- חכמה, ,wisdom– יthe letter ה, the letters ה – ו against the spheres of **foundation** and **kingdom** .those two letters are the last letters ה-ו, in the namesחנוכה סוכה.

The letters of the name **GOD** י-ה-ו-ה - **are identical to the letters of** חנוכה. The letter י indicates to – חכמהwisdom, which is represented by the letter י of **GOD** name, the letter נin the name חנוכהindicates to the sphere of **understanding** - בינהwhich has **fifty** gates ,**fifty** the gematria of the letter נ the second letter in the word חנוכה .

The third letter **in** חנוכה,the letter ו, against the third letter ו,in the name of **GOD.**י-ה-ו-ה which indicates to the spheres representing the attribute **foundation,**The letter כ,in the word חנוכה indicates to the sphere of כתר,which the letter כ represent according to our Rabbis in tractate Sabbath (104, b).

The sphere of the **crown** is represented in stork on the letter י in the name of **GOD** - י-ה-ו-ה.The last letter of חנוכה is the letter ה, against the last letter ה, in the name of **GOD,** representing the sphere of **kingdom**, which represents this world.

There is an important teaching in this order for man's life, starting with **wisdom – חכמה**, acquiring knowledge, then to **understanding** it properly, and practicing it in life.

Another connection of the name חנוכהto the name **GOD** י-ה-ו-ה - is in the small gematria, in which only the digits are counted, the gematria of **is** חנוכה like **GOD** name.8+5+6+2+5-) חנוכה.י-ה-ו-ה 26= 10+5+6+5)-י-ה-ו-ה (,26=.) The smallest gematria of חנוכה is **Eight** (2+6=8).

THE MEANING OF THE NUMBER EIGHT

The number **eight** in Hebrew is – שמנה‎**Eight** is the number which represent the super natural ,**GOD** of miracles which were in **Chanukah**. The letters of the number **eight is** שמנה‎in Hebrew, the same letters as the word **the oil**- השמן‎, oil represent the super natural, as if floats on the water, which represent the material. **Israel** being led in a super natural way by GOD is indicated in the full gematria of the letters of the word **Israel** with the five lettersגוך, מם, שין Oil ישראל‎ 546=360+80+106,) שמן‎,.)

Another Kabbalistic explanation on the name **Chanukah** חנוכה‎, as brought in the book) קהלת יעקב‎kehilat yakov) ,the letters , חנוכה‎can be divided to חנה כו‎, both indicate to the names of **GOD** ,חנה‎gematria **sixty three** (8+50+5=63),and the (26) the name of י-ה-ו-ה‎ .

The number sixty-three is the gematria of the full name of **GOD**-63=20+15+15+13+15) - יה-ו-ה יוד,הי,ואו,הי‎), the name of **GOD** connected with the world of **creation**. Both names of **GOD**, **63** and **26** (63+26=89) ,e qual the Gematria of (8+50+6+20+5=89) חנוכה‎ **Chanukah**.

The world of **creation** in Kabala, is connected with the sphere of **understanding** בינה‎. The sphere of ,**understanding** בינה‎-is the source גבורה‎-**strength** - **Judgment**, these two names of **Mercy** and **Judgment** are connected to **Chanukah** as the other gematria, as we saw before. It is interesting to note, that the number of verses in the portion Naso, in the book Numbers, about the dedication of the Tabernacle is Eighty-**Nine**, like the gematria of **Chanukah**-89) חנוכה‎), as we saw before.

The other part of ,כו חנכה the letters כו in gematria is **26,** as the gematria of **the name of GOD** 26=10+5+6+10)י-ה-ו-ה) the name of GOD, representing **Mercy** and **Loving-Kindness.**

The gematria like **Chanukah** (89) is the combination of the letters ,**the Grace of GOD-** א-ל,- חן(89=58+31) the name of **GOD** א-ל,- represent the attribute Loving-**kindness**,as we saw connected with **Chanukah.**

The commentator **Chida** (in his book Devash Lephi) point out that the two names of GOD אדני – י-ה-ו-ה, representing **Mercy** a festival in which those two attributes of **GOD** were shown to the world.

As we saw before, the Gematria of those two names of **GOD** is **AMEN,**אמן- the root of the word – **EMUNA**אמונה-which is the basis of *Chanukah.*

ANOTHER CONNECTION OF CHANUKAH AND SUKKOTH

Another connection of **Sukkoth** to **Chanukah**, according to Bnei Ysaschar who says that **Sukkoth** and **Chanukah** are connected to our forefather **Jacob**, who died on **Sukkoth**, and was buried in **Chanukah**, **seventy** day from **Sukkoth** to **Chanukah**.

The number **seventy** represents full expansion, like seventy nations etc. The connection of **Jacob** to **Sukkoth** is seen in the verse (Genesis.33, 17) "**ויעקב נסע סוכה**""-and Jacob went out to **Sukkoth**".

Another interesting connection of **Jacob** to **Chanukah** and **Sukkoth** appears in the gematria of the two words **חנוכה –סוכה**-182=89+91+2)) the same gematria as the name **Jacob יעקב-**182=10+70+100+2)).

The connection of **Jacob** to **Chanukah,** is indicated in the struggle that **Jacob** had with the **angel,** the heavenly minister of **Esau.** This struggle took place, when **Jacob** forgot his **jug of oil**, when he took his children over the the river **Yabok.** According to some commentators, this **jug of oil** was the jug that remained with pure olive oil, with which they lit the **Menorah**, in the Temple in **Chanukah.**

CHANUKAH AND THE NAME ISRAEL

In the end, on dawn time, **Jacob** won, and the angel gave him the name **Israel-ישראל**, meaning, **wining the fight with an angel.** This struggle with the angel indicates according to commentators to the struggle of the **Hasmonean** with the **Greeks,** and their victory.

The name ישראל-**Israel** connected to **Chanukah** is seen in the last letter of the full letters of **Chanukah**ישראל ,חנוכה (-30+1+200+300+10=541) .ת,נ,ו,ך,ה,- 5+80+6+50+400=541), י,חי ת,נו נ,ו וכ ך,הה;(The connection of **Chanukah** to the source of **Israel** forefathers, is indicated in the full gematria of the letters with the word, **638**=1+13+408+106+100+10) חנוכה ,נון,ואו,כף,הה) as the gematria of 248+208+182=638)) . אברהם יצחק יעקבInteresting to note, that If we will do the gematria of the letter חית, ח, with the letter ח,חית, י and the letter,ה, ה'י, we will have the gematria, six **hundred and fifty two,** as אברהם יצחק יעקב דוד the four wheels of the **divine chariot.**

HINTS TO CHANUKAH IN THE SRUGLE OF JACOB WITH THE AGEL

Hitting **Jacob** by the angel on Jacob thigh, had effect on the children of **Jacob** on **Chanukah**. The כף-- **thigh**, that was hit by the angel, with the victory of **Jacob**, over the angel changed it to**Jug** - - פך (the letters כף backwards. That was the Jug that Jacob forgot, and return to take back, which brought to the struggle with **Esau** angel. This **Jug of**- פך **oil**, was the **Jug**, that was found in the temple and il brought to the פך (opposite of כף) **jug**, of the oil for the **Menorah**, on **Chanukkah**.

Interesting hint in the Torah, to **Chanukah**, is the word **light** – אור in **beginning** of Torah, which is the **twenty fifth** word, indicating to **Chanukah** which is in the **twenty Fifth** day in the month of **Kislev**. Interesting verse in scriptures about **Light** which contains **twenty fife** letters, is, the verse, " **"כי עמך מקור חיים באורך נראה אור"**." **For with you is the fountain of life; in your light we see light**". (Psalm, 36.10).

The letters 25) כה) are very important letters, as the letter כ, according to the tractate **Shabbat** (104, b) represent the **sphere** כתר - **crown**, the letter ה, is the letter with which this world was created, so that the word, כה represent very high level of divinity, this idea is indicted in the word שכינה- **divine glory**, which is built from the words שכן- כה **place of the dwelling** כה.

THE SECRET OF THE NUMER TWENTY FIVE

According to books of **Kabbalah** the number **twenty-five,** being half of the number **fifty**, represents the midst of the way to the highest level of **heaven,** the **fifty gate** of heaven, the sphere of כתר,- **crown**. The כהן contains the letters, כה נ represent his destiny to elevate the people to the high level. of the .**fifty** - נ

A deeper connection of the light of the beginning of the world, **the hidden light,** the **light that** was concealed because of the wicked people who would misuse it. This light will shine in the end of days to the righteous people.

According to the Rabbis, this light lights in the light of **Chanukah candles**. The candles of **Chanukah** are connected to the candles of the **Menora**h in the temple, whose light is from **Hidden Light**.

THE GREAT SANCTITY OF CHANUKAH

The great sanctity of **Chanukah** is seen from the gematria of the words חג חנוכה - **the festival of Chanukah**, (11+89=100). Hundred, is the numerical value of the letter ק,. the letter which representקדושה - ,**sanctity** as the tractate **Shabbat** (104b) says. In order to get holiness, our Rabbis established the law to say **hundred** blessings, every day, against the -Sam-100) סמ) the evil part of the angle .Samuel **סמאל** - Saying Hundred blessing every day, strength man belief in **GOD**. the Belief that the festival of **Chanukah** does.

The **Zohar** says that the letter קוף ,,קwhich means **monkey**, its root from the word הקף, -**surrounding**, represent external things..Hundred as we saw, is the gematria of the word **Sam- סמ**, the evil part of the name of the evil angel,-**Samael—סמאל-** , the angel that wrestled with **Jacob**, when he went back, to bring the **jug of oil**, this Jug of oil was this one which remained pure in was used for **Chanukah.**

The festival of **Chanukah,** as we saw, represents the victory of **Jacob** on the angel. The round shape of the letters **סמ**, the negative letters of the name, **סמאל**, indicating to the external forces. The numerical value of the letters **סמ** is **100,** like the numerical value of the letter ק.

Interesting to note, that the root of the word קוףIs הקף surrounding.

קוף, in Hebrew is monkey which represent imitation, as the Zohar calls the evil forces קוף , because they **copy** their ideas from the true values of the Torah and translate it to materialistic matters.

This is the characteristic of the **Greeks** philosophy, especially of Aristotle.The evil of Greeks is seen in the same gematria of מלך יון Te king **GREEC** (90 +66 =156) **Antiyochos** -1+50+10+6) אנטיוכס

156   =60+   20+). The same gematria as **Zion-** ציון
156=90+10+6+50)), and Joseph- 156= 10+6+60+80)יוסף).

THE CONNECTION OF JOSEF AND CHANUKAH

The connection of יוסף and, **Chanukah** – חנוכה is indicated in the letters of the words of the words והכן טב"ח as the verse says in Genesis (43,16,) "**Slaughter and prepare**", in connection with the feast that **Joseph** prepared for his brothers as the full verse says, "**Take these men to my house", slaughter an animal and prepare a meal; as they are going to eat with me <u>at noon</u>.**"

The men are the brothers of **Joseph**, and **Joseph** ordered it for them. The relevance of the verse to **Chanukah,** is explained by the words of the Talmud that **Joseph** here, ordered that the **forbidden sinew** of the animal be removed. The commandment of removing the forbidden **sinew**, reminds us of the struggle between **Jacob** and the ministering angel of **Esau,** struggle in which this **tendon of Jacobs** leg was injured.

This injury, according to our sages, was a prophecy of a coming destruction, which was to be caused by the ministering angel of Esau in the generation of the **Hellenists.** During this era, multitudes of Jews were either slaughter or Hellenized.

The removal of the forbidden sinew is therefore seen as are rectification of this damage. Overcoming the satanic powers which threaten to demolish Israel, is embodied by **Joseph,** for he withstood the temptation from committing an immoral act in **Egypt.** The victory of Jacob on the Satan, is indicated according to the Chatam Sofer, in the numerical value of the words,541=182+359) יעקב - שטן)is like the numerical value of the word **Israel**-ישראל.Indicating to name **Israel**, which according to the **Torah** means "**ruling over the angel**," שרר על א-ל"."".

Indication to this victory of Israel in **Chanukah,** is in the last letters of the full letters –חנוכהChanukah חית,נונ,ואו,כף,הה–ת-נ-ו-ף-ה- ,ישראל-(541=400+50+6+80+5) 541=10+300+200+1+30)).

This righteous strength was transmitted to the children of Israel, whom Scripture calls "the remnant of **Joseph** ". It is the same strength which enabled **Matityahu** and the rest of the **Hasmoneans** to rid the Temple of the Greek impurity.

According to Tana Debei Eliyahu it indicates to the power of Joseph the righteous on latter generations as it came out on Chanukah. Joseph who manages to keep his righteousness in Egypt gave the power to the Harmonium in Greece.

MEANING OF THE WORDS ZION AND YAVAN

Their victory, as we saw before, is shown in the letters of the word **Zion - ציון**. As we saw, the numerical value of the word156) **יוסף**) is the same gematria as **יוסף** ,(156=90+10+6+50)**Zion**ציון - 156=10+6+60+80)).

Chanukah is alluded in the verse "**ועוררתי בניך ציון על בניך יוון**," ‚**„And I will incite your sons, Zion, upon your sons, Greece"** (Zachariah, 9,13) This teaches us about **Joseph** righteousness, which awakened within the people of Israel at the time of the **Greek**. Idea which is revealed by the equivalent numerical values of **יוסף**, and**ציון** as we saw before.

The victory of the Righteous **Matityahu** and sons, on **Greek,** is shown in the letters of the word - **ציון** Zion, in which the letter **צ** **צדיק**meaning **righteous**- over the letters **יון**-Greek, indicating to the victory of the **Righteous** over **Greek**. The built up of the word **ציון** **צ-יון**, that **Zion** who represents the **Torah,** swallowed the wisdom of **Greek** as we saw before. **Zion,** is the source of Torah as is written "**כי**" **מציון תצא תורה** "**Out of Zion Torah will come out**" ,(Isiah,2,3)

The number, **hundred and fifty six**, is also the Gematria of the word - **קנאה**Jealousy,(100+1+50+1+5=156) signifying that the **Jealousy** which is aroused against impurity, has its source in the righteous person, and this is a basic quality within the soul of **Israel**. The letters of the root of the word - **קנאה**Jealousy, **קנא** - which have the same letters of the word **נקא,**, similar to the word **נקה**meaning **clean**, or **pure**, teaching us, that it is the **cleaning** and **purifying** of the soul, which gives rise to the righteous **jealousy**.

This phenomenon was exemplified by the struggle of the **Hasmoneans**, in which the sons of **Zion** revolted against the sons of **Greece**.

On **Chanukah**, as on **Succoth**, the power of vision plays an important role. The Talmudic scholars said in the Gemara that the Mitzvah of the **Sukkah**, is fulfilled by sitting under the shade, and seeing, the roof, **Schach**, (the branches) etc, the roof of the Sukkah). Similarly, on **Chanukah** is great importance to see the light of the candles, and one who simply observes the light of candles may say a blessing.

The **Chanukah** candles, containing **oil, wick, fire**; represent the different parts of the man's soul. The letters of the word נר (lamp. candle) indicates to the) נפשlower level of the soul) and the רוח)middle level of the soul), and) נשמהa higher level of the soul). Its connection to the Soul, is shown by the letters of השמן (the oil) which have same letters as the word) , נשמהthe highest part of the soul, (in man).

THE SYMBOL OF OIL AND THE WICK AND THE FIRE

The flame, emitted by the wick, symbolizes the **hidden light**, which illuminates the hearts of Israel on **Chanukah** .Even souls which occupy the lowest merit the blessing of this illumination. This is learned from the Talmudic sage, who say that **oils,** and **wicks,** which are unfit for use for **Sabbath,** are nevertheless, acceptable for use on **Chanukah.**

Sabbath, requires spiritual preparation, in order for man to attain its holiness, not so on **Chanukah.**

THE GREAT LIGHT OF CHANUKKAH

The reason for it, is that on **Chanukah** it is the holy light which penetrates even, through the dense materialistic curtain. All this became possible through the utter devotion of the **Hasmoneans**, a devotion which had the power to endow even ordinary secular weekdays, with light and holiness. The light of **Chanukah** is a light which comes out from darkness, and this is the enigma of all lights, the fact that it stems originally, from a void abyss.

The verse in Scripture reads, "**העם ההולכים בחושך ראו אור גדול**" "**The people who walked in darkness have seen great light**", (Isaiah 9:1) From out of darkness, springs out light that shatters this very thick darkness. The **נר**, **Candle,** which symbolizes the soul, also symbolizes the **two hundred and forty-eight, positive** commandments, in combination with the qualities of **love** and **fear**, qualities which according to the **Zohar**, elevate the commandments to heaven like the two wings of the bird. Love and Fear of GOD must accompany the Commandments in order to bring them to perfection.

wings of the bird, through which she can go high, so, serving God with fear and love elevate a person to high spiritual worlds is basically like the fire of the candle. Fire which completes the function the candle. So, love and peace of GOD. This idea comes out from the numerical value of the word **candle -נר** which equals 250 (200 +50=250) against the 248 positive commandments, and the two qualities, Love and Fear. which complete the function of the soul.. Candle **נר**thus, represents the perfection of the commandments. This is similar to the vessels used for receiving the light of the Torah.**נר** which represent the Torah as is written **כי**" "**אור ותורה מצוה נר** ,"**As the Candle is the Commandment and theTorah is the light.**"

THE LIGHT OF CHANUKKAH AND THE TORAH

The connection of the **candle** and **Torah**, is expressed in the full gematria, of the word, 616 =106+510) **נר נון, ריש**) which is the same gematria as the word **The Torah**-611=5+400+200+6+5) **התורה**).The **two hundred and forty eight** positive commandments together with the two attributes of **Love** and Fear of **God** –adds to the number **two hundred and fifty, as** ,the gematria of the word **candle– נר**. Those two attributes, **Love** and **Fear** of **GOD**, complete the Torah as it sin in the full gematria of the word, The **Torah תורה**, and the full gematria in the word .**candle– נר**

On the eighth. day of **Chanukah**, eight lamps radiate the light of **Torah**. **Sukkoth** and **Chanukah** are similar in this respect as well, as we will see.

The last day of **Sukkoth**, **Shemini Atzeret**, is designated as a time for celebrating the privilege of having the **Torah**. On this day the light of the Torah, which brings happiness and joy to the soul, is revealed, as the psalm tell us. **פקודי ה' ישרים משמחי לב** ," "" , " **The statutes of God are upright, making the heart joyful**" (psalms,19,9).

Sukkoth like **Chanukah** lights, indicates in its name, to the holiness of the commandment, so it is in the commandment of **סוכה**)Sukkah). The full gematria of the letters of the word, **סמד, ויו, כף,**" 248=120+22+100+6) **הא**),which adds up to the numerical value two hundred and forty-eight, corresponding to the two **hundred and forty-eight** positive commandments.

Consequently, the fact that the gematria of Sukkah, equal the number. **two hundred and forty**-eight, commandments. shows, that the commandment of the Sukkah, is considered equal, to the holiness to the **two hundred and forty-eight**, positive mitzvoth of the **Torah**.

The commandments of **Sukkoth** are the instruments, which allow to the light of **Torah**, to shine in all its brilliance on **Shemini Atzereth** in **Sukkoth**.This is similar to the **eighth day** of **Chanuka**, which is called - **זאת חנוכה** This is Chanukah ,which is the climax of all the days of **Chanukah**.

The similarity between the last day of **Chanukah,** and the last day of **Sukkoth,** which is **Shemini Atzeret,** both the days of these holidays are considered as the pinnacle, which embodies the essence of the entire holiday. The eighth divine attribute In **Kabala** is the sphere - **understanding**בינה, which influences the seven attributes on the scale beneath it.

The existence of the soul is dependent upon **understanding**, as it is written ""**נשמת ש-די תבינם**" "...**and the soul of the Almighty which gives them understanding**." (Job, 32,8)

The connection between the Soul and understanding, the eighth attribute, is also expressed through the letters of the word **soul**- נשמה, which are the same in the word **Eight** - שמנה.

THE MEANING OF THE NAME OF THE LAST DAY OF CHANUKAH

The last day of Chanukah is very often referred to as," This is Chanukah "זאת חנוכה" ", as in the verse," "וזאת התורה אשר שם משה לפני" בני ישראל "And this is the Torah, which Moses set before the children of Israel…". (Numbers, 4:4)

the letter ז and the letters, א-ת.And the letter, the letter which has a numerical value of **seven**, the number which mystically represent this world, the letters of the **Aleph Bet**, which were the foundation of the world.

The Torah contains keys of the understanding of both worlds. Interesting to note that the numerical value of the words **זאת חנוכה** 497=408+89), is like the numerical value of the name of festival of **Sukkoth**- 497=11+486,**חג סכות**).(Interesting to note that the number 497 ,the numeral of those festivals is the same like the Sphere **מלכות -Kingdom**   ,the   last   sphere   of   the Spheres,(40+30+20+6+400+1=497).

The day of **Shemini Atzeret**, is also called **שמחת תורה** the **Joy of the Torah**, designated as a time for celebration the privilege of having the **Torah**.

On this day the light of the **Torah**, brings **happens** and **Joy** to the soul, idea which is revealed as in the psalm, **"פקודי ה' ישרים משמחי לב"**, " **The statures of God are upright, making the heart joyful**" (psalms,19,9). **Sukkoth**, like the **Chanukah** lights indicates to the holiness of the commandants, as it is clear from the implications found in the letters of the word **סוכה**as spelled out fully **סמך,וו,כף,הא,** , add up to the numerical value (120+12+100+6=248,) corresponding to the 248 positive commandants. Consequently, the fact that the gematria of **Sukkah,** is 248, like the number of the positive commandment, shows that the greatness of the commandment of the **Sukkah.**

The commandments of **Sukkoth** are the instruments which allow the light of the **Torah**, to shine in all its brilliance on **Shemini Atzereth**.

The Empire of **Greece** is indicated in the **Torah** according to our Rabbis in the passage **and darkness was on"....""וחשך על פני תהום"**, **face of the depth** ",(Genesis,1:2). The word –**Darkness** -וחשך, refers to **Greece**, which attempted to **darken** the eyes of **Israel**, by obstructing the light of the holy **Torah**.

This is expressed in the prayer of **Chanukah, Al Hanisim**, by the phrase **"to make them forget Your Torah, and to draw them away from the decrees of your will"**.

The darkening of the eyes of Israel, neglecting of Torah, would bring them to forget the Torah, idea which find support by the identical letters of the words שכח (forget) and) חשך darkness).

The power of the **Satan** to make Jews forgetting the Torah, into the nation of **Israel**, according to our sages, through the wound which Esau's ministering angel caused to the sinew in Jacobs's leg. A wound, which caused in the history is persecution of Jews, in the later generation, when Israel suffered during the reigns of their many oppressive conquerors.

According to the **Zohar, גיד הנשה** (the sinew of the thigh muscle) is from the word נשיה, which means forgetting שכח-, hinting to the power the **Satan** to cause Israel to forget the Torah and forsake the service of G-d. Another explanation for the word) גיד הנשה femoral sinew) related to the word) נשים women). Rabbi Samson Raphael Hirsh explains that from this relationship, we may view the wound inflicted on Jacob by the **Satan**, as a manifestation of the evil inclination, in the form in the lust for women.

According to the Zohar, during the days of **Greek's** rule, many Jews were accused of not obeying the laws of circumcision. The commentator, Sham Mishmuel explains, that the sin mentioned by the **Zohar**, was actually the marriage of Jewish men to non-Jewish women.

As the sages say that a man who intermarries, encourages abets the continuity of non-circumcision.

This is the sin which **Greece** forced upon the people of Israel. This defect in Israel was the result of the damage caused by **Esau's** heavenly minister, to Jacob's femoral sinew. It is Interesting to note that the gematria of the word,377=17+360) גיד הנשה) is the same as the gematria of **Esau**, עשו –with the total (70+300+6+1=377), Esau and the formal sinew. also has the gimariaLeft- – שמאול 377=300+40+1+6+30)).

The two connotations of the **word**, נשה one of) נשיהforgetting), and one of) נשיםwomen) have definite correlation in that we are told by our holy sources that the abandonment of the covenant of circumcision, causes deterioration of the memory.

This is because) זכרremember)is for the language denoting זך)pure) ריש) ,ר) the letter Rר-- represents the Headראש-, purity being a result of the זכיות-**merits** of the soul which its place it in the head. The word 377=70+300+6+1) עשו) with the word, has the same gematria of the is like 377=17+360) גיד הנשה).

Darkness, according to our Sages, represents the materialistic world, of lust and materialistic desires which cause a man to forget his creator, and forsake His commandment.

ANOTHER MEANING TO THE WORD CHANUKAH

The word - חנוכה Chanukah comes from the term) חנוך education, or training for vocation), teaching us that Israel accepted the yoke of the kingdom of Heaven, with love and enthusiasm, as one who is initiated into the service of God. Similarity, on **Chanukah** a man is provided with incentive to accept new challenges and responsibilities for the service of God, as the days of **Chanukah** are favorable for this.

The similarity between **Chanukah** and **Sukkoth** is also expressed by the fact that the last day of **Sukkoth** which is **Shmini Atzert,** and the last day of **Chanukah** represent the **climax** of the days of each respective holiday.

The word) חשמונאים Hasmoneans) is a name built from the letters חשמ , indicates to the three measures, through which the **Greeks** tried to destroy the Jewish religion :) חדש month) ,) שבת Sabbath)and מילה)circumcision) .

These three commandments are the backbone of the Jewish belief and are essential for the continuance of Israel. The sanctification of each new month exhibits Israel's power to make holy these particular periods of time, and the forces of nature active within them.

The holiness of the **Sabbath** cleanses man and liberates him from the forces of nature, for on **Sabbath**, man refrains from tampering with, or altering the processes of nature. Also, Israel must continue to observe the covenant of circumcision, for it is a ritual which purifies and sanctifies both body and soul.

The **Greeks** wanted to obliterate these practices from Jewish life, for they did not believe in the holiness of the supreme forces which sustain the world. This holiness is, however, based upon the three foundations we just mentioned: (sanctification of the month), earth (sabbatical rejuvenation of nature), and the soul (purification through circumcision).

Chanukah proves clearly the power which our wise sages possessed, for they were able to implant the secular days with the holiness of the festival, a holiness which the **Greeks** tried to erase.

The three foundations of holy existence, and their preservation throughout the dark days of exile, constituted the primary work of **Joseph**, while he was in Egypt. **Joseph,** primary work of while he was in Egypt, **Joseph** toiled to keep this holiness alive, as our sages tell us that he observed **Sabbath**, while he was in **Egypt**, and even upheld the commandment of circumcision. In fact, Joseph not only kept this covenant of circumcision himself, but convinced the Egyptians to become circumcised. Joseph's adherence to the three rudimentary foundations of the holy existences, hinted at by the verse **חמש את מצרים**" he **equipped the land of Egypt**".

The early scholars point out that the letters of the word **חמש** ("he equipped") form the acrostic **חדש, מילה שבת,** implying that **Joseph** introduced these three elements into the Egyptian culture.

On **Chanukah**, the Torah portion, which is read, deals with the **dedication** of the Holy **Tabernacle** by the princes of Israel. These princes also contributed to the continuation of the holy light in this world by offering their sacrifices. The vessels brought by the princes included twelve silver dishes, twelve silver bowels, and twelve golden spoons, all together equaling to thirty-six vessels. This corresponds to the thirty days of **Chanukah**, and to **thirty-six** righteous men in every generation, upon whom the world 's existence depends.

The Sfath Emeth says, that these **thirty-six** righteous men should be understood in relation to the **thirty-six** times that the Torah mentions words connected with light, hinting to the hidden light, which lighted to Adam, for **thirty-six** hours.

This light is revealed also by the **thirty-six** candles, which are lit on **Chanukah**. Just as the princes perpetuated this light with their sacrifices, so did the Hasmoneans, through their unwavering loyalty, brought this light to the commandment of the Chanukah candles.

The illumination of **Chanukah** according to Rabbi Tzadok Hkoen continues on **Sabbath** throughout the year, and with respect to this feature. **Chanukah** is the initiator of the light presented on **Sabbath**. This is the reason says Rabbi Tzadock, that the laws and matters of **Chanukah** are dealt with in the tractate **Sabbath..** The holy light of **Sabbath** draws its strength from the light of of **Chanukkah**, the **hidden light**.

Rabbi Tzadok Hkohen maintains that within the **Oral Law** is hidden this eternal illumination, as we saw about the connection of the **thirty-six** tractates, like the **thirty-six** of **Chanukah** candles in which the **Hidden light** which lighted **thirty-six** hours in the beginning of the creation.

The **Oral Law** is the equivalent according to the Kabbalah, to the holy attribute of **dominion -** מלכות, the dominion of the mouth and speech. Similarly, **Sabbath** the seventh day, corresponds to dominion, which is the **seventh** attribute.

The connection of the **thirty six** hours of the **hidden light** is indicated in the numerical value, of five times the word – אור**light**, appearing in the beginning of the creation. **Five** times) אור light) equal **1035** (207x5=1035) according the kabbalist Rabbi Isaac Luria **1000** אלף -is like **one** א.אלף,, so, that the number **1035** -35 +1=36).showing that in the first **thirty six** hours of creation, the original light of creation, was the **Hidden light** ,that because of the wicked people who will misuse it, it was hidden.

These five times the word **Light,** are against the five books of Moses and against the part of the **soul**נפש, רוח, נשמה, חיה, יחידה..Against these five, the Greeks did five decrees against Israel, circumcision, sanctification of the new

moon, Sabbath, studying **Torah,** saying that the do not have any part in **GOD.**

The main letters of the name חשמונאי-חשמ, the letters of the number חמש , **five. The letters חמש-** are also the abbreviation of the main decrees of the **Greeks** חודש, **שבת,מילה,** **Circumcision Sabbath, and** the **Sanctification of the new moon .**

Interesting explanation why the **Greeks** decreed mainly against these three decrees, is given. It is known that the planets Saturn Mars, and the Moon has negative influence on the world. Against these negative forces of the plants, Jew got three commandment, circumcision which is against the plant **Mars**, which to do with blood, **Sabbath** (Saturday) against **Saturn**, the **Sanctification** of the moon, against the negative influence of the **Moon**.

The **Greeks** wanted that the Jews will be affected by those plants; therefore, they forbade them to keep these commandments.

TU B'SHVAT

*

TU B'AV

*

PURIM

Introduction

In the realm of Jewish festivals, there exists a collection of sacred occasions that hold within them the potential to unlock the hidden depths of our souls. Tu b'Shvat, Tu b'Av, and Purim – three enchanting celebrations intricately woven into the fabric of Jewish culture, history, and spirituality. These festivals, seemingly separate and distinct, come alive in their shared essence when viewed through the lens of Kabbalah, the mystical tradition of Judaism.

"The Mystical Tapestry: Exploring Tu b'Shvat, Tu b'Av & Purim through Kabbalah and Hebrew Letters" is an immersive journey into the heart of these extraordinary festivals. Guided by the ancient wisdom of Kabbalah and the mystical power embedded within the Hebrew letters, this book invites you to embark on a transformative exploration, unearthing the profound teachings and spiritual significance that lie beneath the surface.

Through the pages of this captivating work, you will be transported to the captivating world of Tu b'Shvat – the New Year for Trees. Discover how this festival, traditionally associated with nature and the cycles of growth, can illuminate the path to our own personal growth and spiritual nurturing. Unlock the wisdom encoded within the Hebrew letters, allowing the spiritual teachings of Tu b'Shvat to blossom within your heart and guide you towards a deeper connection with the divine.

As you continue your journey, the tapestry unfolds to reveal the captivating festival of Tu b'Av – a celebration of love, unity, and connection. Delve into the profound symbolism and hidden meanings of Tu b'Av, unraveling the mysteries of love, relationships, and the unification of souls. Through the mystical interpretations of Kabbalah and the intricate dance of Hebrew letters, discover how Tu b'Av can serve as a beacon of light in the realm of personal relationships, fostering a deeper understanding and harmony between individuals.

Finally, the journey reaches its crescendo with the festival of Purim – an epic tale of courage, redemption, and triumph over darkness. Dive into the enigmatic world of Purim where spiritual battles and divine interventions intertwine, as you uncover the veiled truths of your existence and awaken to your own hidden potentials. Through the Kabbalistic interpretations of Purim's ancient teachings and the transformative power of Hebrew letters, come face to face with the triumphant dance of light over darkness, and embrace the magic that unfolds within your own soul.

"The Mystical Tapestry" is not merely a book; it is an invitation. An invitation to venture beyond the surface and dive headfirst into the depths of these festivals. With each turn of the page, expect to encounter practices, rituals, meditations, and insights that will ignite the flame of divine connection within you. Allow the harmonious blend of ancient wisdom and contemporary understanding to guide you towards self-discovery, spiritual growth, and a profound sense of interconnectedness with all that exists.

May this exploration awaken your soul, expand your consciousness, and deepen your understanding of the intricate tapestry of creation. Embrace the transformative power of Tu b'Shvat, Tu b'Av, and Purim through the profound teachings of Kabbalah and the sacred language of Hebrew letters. Step into the mystical tapestry and let the enchantment of these festivals guide you on a journey of self-discovery and connection with the divine.

TU B'SHVAT

TU B'SHVAT

The Seasonal Significance of Tu b'Shvat

Tu b'Shvat, (The fifteenth in the month *Shvat*) the beginning of the year for trees according to *the Rabbis of the House of Rabbi Hillel*, is a time when the majority of the seasonal rains come.

The blossoming of flowers and fruits is a result of the blessings that this floral New Year brings. The wells in which these rains are stored are full at this time of year, as indicated by the astrological sign of the month *Shvat*, the pail (or Aquarius).

The month of *Shvat*, which heralds the influx of abundant waters into the world, is also a time when the waters of the Torah are released into the world.

This is seen from the Torah itself, which states that on the first of the month of **Shvat** Moses began to give his final admonition to the Children of Israel, as recorded in the book Deuteronomy: "And it came to pass, in the fortieth year, in the eleventh month, on the first day of the month that Moses spoke unto the Children of Israel according unto all that the Lord had given him in commandment unto them.

The Words of Torah, which are often metaphorically referred to as rain, were granted to Israel at the beginning of the month of **Shvat**.

The words of the Torah were spoken through the mouth of Moses in the form of ethical counsel and reprimands. Contained in his orations were ideas of hope, redemption, consolation, and comfort.

All these ideas were expressed by repeating God's words in Deuteronomy. According to our honored sages, this repetition provides us with tools to enable us to discover the intended messages hidden within the Oral Law.

The meaning of the name of the month שבט (*Shvat*), according to Rabbi *Tzadok Hakohen*, comes from the term שבט meaning striking stick, or even שוט "**whip**". since the letters ו and the letter ב are from the group of labial letters that are interchangeable.

This association affords support for what is written in the Medrash *Pesikta Zutratha* that at this time of the year the ten plagues (or, according to another opinion, the last three plagues, those which had the most profound effect on Pharaoh's heart) began to descend upon Egypt; and the faith of the Children of Israel was strengthened as they watched the hand of God inflict punishment upon the Egyptians.

During the same period, forty years later, Moses began rebuking the Children of Israel themselves very harshly for their sins.

The season during which the fruit trees bud and blossom coincides with the period during which Israel blossomed into a Torah nation, for as we explained, the Torah was given around the time when the trees yield their first fruits.

Fruit trees were man's main source of physical sustenance before Adam's sin. We may discern certain similarities between the stages of development through which the first fruits pass and those which Israel underwent during their evolution into a Torah nation.

The material and spiritual food of man is totally dependent on each other, as the rabbis of the Talmud emphasized, "If there is no flour there is no Torah, and if there is no Torah there is no flour."

This principle forms a reality of nature, for God created this world using the Torah as His model.

When Opportunity Ripens

The New Year for the fruit trees is in a sense a form of rectification of Adam's sin of eating from the tree of knowledge.

This concept finds expression during this time of year in the eating of many different kinds of fruit, and especially the seven main species for which the Land of Israel is praised.

According to many opinions, the Tree of knowledge was just one of these seven species, and according to others, the fruit from this tree tasted of all seven species.

Eating fruits on the new year of trees in holiness and innocence cleanses and purifies them from the foulness of the serpent which has contaminated them ever since Adam's sin.

The restoration of these fruits to their original state is completed on the day the Torah was given, which also is the day when the first fruits were offered to God. During the time when the Temple stood, two loaves of leavened bread were brought on this day to be offered unto the Lord.

The offering of these loaves symbolized the rectification of Adam's sin, since the tree of knowledge is considered to have produced certain types of wheat.

The leaven within the loaves represented the evil inclination, sublimated and humbled into accepting the holiness of Torah and even aiding man in demonstrating his devotion to the Holy One.

This is the ultimate achievement in man's existence, for it is written in Scripture לעבדך בכל לבבך ("...**and to serve him with your whole heart**"). The extra letter ב in the word לבבכם (your heart) reminds us that we must dedicate both the good and the evil inclinations of our hearts to the service of God.

The damage caused by Adam's sin of eating from the Tree of knowledge is repaired on *Tu b'Shvat*. Rabbi *Tzadok Hakohen* claims that this idea is expressed by the letter צ. He notes that, according to the Book of Creation, the month of *Shvat* was created with the letter צ.

It is also the letter representing צדיק, the righteous person, who is characterized, among other things, by the fact that he eats in holiness, as the verse tells us, "The righteous one eats until his soul is sated." The Book of Creation uses the expression, ""The month of *Shvat* was created with the letter צ...," suggesting that the improvement in habits of eating is the main task of man during the month of *Shvat*. This is shown by the theme of the central holiday of this month, Tu *b'Shvat*.

The repentance and setting aright of Adam's sin, according to our holy books, comes through the study of the Oral Law, for the Oral Law contains ample wisdom to appease God's righteous anger, as King Solomon indicates in Ecclesiastes: "where there is more wisdom there are more wraths."

The connotation of filling oneself with the waters of the Torah, which this sign contains, came to expression in the history of the Jewish people. This is particularly true of the Oral tradition. The main attributes of the Oral tradition are symbolized in the letter of the month, the *Tzadi*, whose form consists of the combination of the letters *Yod* and Nun, symbolizing wisdom and understanding (see *Pri Tzadik*, Exodus, *Shvat*).

The *Yod* and the *Nun* also symbolize the essential unity of the written and Oral traditions: the *Yod*, symbolizing wisdom, and stands for the written Torah, and the Nun, symbolizing understanding, stands for the Oral Torah.

Rabbi *Tzadok* explains that the analogy between the Torah and water applies mainly to the Oral Torah. He cites the verse ", All ye who thirst, come to water," on which our sages explain that it refers to the Torah.

Interesting to note the bucket (דלי), is the sign of the zodiac of this month, symbolizing Israel whom Israel drew water, and gave the other, as this is the goal of as GOD said to the Jews on mountain Sini, you will be a kingdom of priests whose task is to teach.

Israel's essential purpose of Creation is to serve God through the Torah, compared to water; "water" is none other than Torah.

The level of the *Tzadik*, the righteous one, is the natural level of Israel, as it is written (Isaiah, chapter. 60,v. 21): "And your nation is entirely righteous, they will inherit the land forever."

The bucket of water is the sign of Israel because its sole purpose is to draw water, water is a symbol for Torah, as we saw. This indicates that Israel's essential purpose of Cr creation is to serve God through the Torah,

This verse refers to the Oral Law, according to the *Bnei Isaschar*, which requires long and tedious hours of study. This study purifies man from the defilement of Adam's sin.

It is the Oral Law that was revealed in Deuteronomy by Moses from the first day of *Shvat*, the time of abundant waters on the earth.

The purification of the body which the Oral Law affects is seen in the holy and pure

eating which is revealed within the profound meaning of Tu *b'Shvat*, the new year for fruit trees.

The tree symbolizes the written Torah, and its fruit symbolizes the Oral tradition, which draws its sustenance from the written Torah just as a fruit draws sustenance from the tree.

Here we find a clear example of how the physical parallels the spiritual (see *Chidushei HaRim, Tu b'Shvat*). According to the *Chidushei HaRim* (ibid.), the name Shvat is related to the word *shofet* (judge), because during this month one receives divine judgment on the spiritual sustenance of the whole year, for the capacity of originality in understanding the Oral tradition.

This parallels the fact that the fifteenth of *Shvat* is the New Year's Day fortress when the judgment on the quality and quantity of the next year's produce is divinely ordained.

The fact that this month is the source of inspiration for new ideas in the Torah may also explain the astrological prognostication that Aquarians are creative, because of the principle that when the wellsprings are opened they flow in two directions: to the spiritual wisdom of the Torah, and to the natural wisdom of the sciences. In fact, the *Zoahar* predicted that there would be a great opening of the wellsprings of wisdom continuing from the year 1840) 5600 - ה'תר B.C.E.) onward.

Beginning at that time, we noticed a significant increase of wisdom, both spiritual and secular. The name *Shvat* is also related to the word *poshet* (מתפשט), meaning spreading out, which denotes the spread of the influence of wisdom during the month of *Shvat*.

The month of *Shvat* is a time when anybody, no matter how far he is from holiness, may easily come closer to God and renew himself by detaching himself from his sinful past (Shem MiShmuel, *Shemot*, Va'erah).

Similar prognostications are made by the science of astrology for those born under the sign of Aquarius, who note the energy of fundamental change, a clear break from the past.

In the context of Judaism, these qualities need to bring a person to spiritual renewal, to complete repentance and liberation from the misdeeds of the past.

The difference between the two halves of the month is also seen in the tribe representing it, Asher, whose land is blessed with olives and oil. According to our Sages, olives eaten alone may sometimes cause forgetfulness, whereas olive oil is good for reinforcing memory.

The difference between the olive and the oil is that the oil is made by squeezing and grinding the olive. Similarly, during the month of *Shvat*, a person may undergo a fundamental change as a result of doing penance after the days of *Shovavim*, which are set aside for repentance.

Tu b'Shvat in Kabbalah

The great Kabbalist Isaac Luria and his disciples in the City Safed initiated what was called **Tu B'shvat Seder** similar to that of the Passover seder.

The idea of this seder is brought in a book called פרי עץ הדר - meaning, Fruit of a beautiful tree, basically refers to the tree of Life.

The basis of Tu B'shvat Seder is Kabalistic to do with spheres, as is seen at the end of the Seder which is said:

"May all sparks scattered by our hands or our ancestors, or by the sin of the first human against the fruits of the tree be returned and included in the majestic might of the Tree of Life.

Kabbalistic Tu B'shvat Seder

נוֹהֲגִים לַעֲרֹךְ אֶת הַשֻּׁלְחָן בְּפֵרוֹת אִילָן. אֲבִי הַמִּשְׁפָּחָה אוֹ עוֹרֵךְ הַסֵּדֶר פּוֹתֵחַ
בְּמָקוֹרוֹ שֶׁל ט"וּ בִּשְׁבָט:

אַרְבָּעָה רָאשֵׁי שָׁנִים הֵם בְּאֶחָד בְּנִיסָן - רֹאשׁ הַשָּׁנָה לַמְּלָכִים וְלָרְגָלִים בְּאֶחָד בֶּאֱלוּל -
רֹאשׁ הַשָּׁנָה לְמַעֲשַׂר בְּהֵמָה בְּאֶחָד בְּתִשְׁרֵי - רֹאשׁ הַשָּׁנָה לַשָּׁנִים וְלִשְׁמִיטִין וְלַיּוֹבְלוֹת,
לִנְטִיעָה וְלִירָקוֹת בְּאֶחָד בִּשְׁבָט - רֹאשׁ הַשָּׁנָה לָאִילָן, כְּדִבְרֵי בֵּית שַׁמַּאי.

בֵּית הַלֵּל אוֹמְרִים בַּחֲמִשָּׁה עָשָׂר בּוֹ!

יִקְחוּ מַאֲכָל הֶעָשׂוּי מִן הַחִטָּה אוֹ שְׂעוֹרָה - כְּגוֹן עוּגוֹת וִיבָרְכוּ עָלָיו:

בָּרוּךְ אַתָּה ה' אֱלֹקֵינוּ מֶלֶךְ הָעוֹלָם בּוֹרֵא מִינֵי מְזוֹנוֹת:

אַחַר שֶׁיֹּאכְלוּ מְעַט יֹאמְרוּ פְּסוּקִים בְּעִנְיַן חִטָּה וְלֶחֶם:

וְשָׁמַרְתָּ אֶת מִצְוֹת יְהוָה אֱלֹהֶיךָ לָלֶכֶת בִּדְרָכָיו וּלְיִרְאָה אֹתוֹ: כִּי יְהוָה אֱלֹהֶיךָ מְבִיאֲךָ
אֶל אֶרֶץ טוֹבָה אֶרֶץ נַחֲלֵי מָיִם עֲיָנֹת וּתְהֹמֹת יֹצְאִים בַּבִּקְעָה וּבָהָר: אֶרֶץ חִטָּה וּשְׂעֹרָה
וְגֶפֶן וּתְאֵנָה וְרִמּוֹן אֶרֶץ זֵית שֶׁמֶן וּדְבָשׁ: אֶרֶץ אֲשֶׁר לֹא בְמִסְכֵּנֻת תֹּאכַל בָּהּ לֶחֶם לֹא
תֶחְסַר כֹּל בָּהּ אֶרֶץ אֲשֶׁר אֲבָנֶיהָ בַרְזֶל וּמֵהֲרָרֶיהָ תַּחְצֹב נְחֹשֶׁת: וְאָכַלְתָּ וְשָׂבָעְתָּ וּבֵרַכְתָּ
אֶת יְהוָה אֱלֹהֶיךָ עַל הָאָרֶץ הַטֹּבָה אֲשֶׁר נָתַן לָךְ: הִשָּׁמֶר לְךָ פֶּן תִּשְׁכַּח אֶת יְהוָה אֱלֹהֶיךָ
לְבִלְתִּי שְׁמֹר מִצְוֹתָיו וּמִשְׁפָּטָיו וְחֻקֹּתָיו אֲשֶׁר אָנֹכִי מְצַוְּךָ הַיּוֹם: פֶּן תֹּאכַל וְשָׂבָעְתָּ
וּבָתִּים טֹבִים תִּבְנֶה וְיָשָׁבְתָּ: וּבְקָרְךָ וְצֹאנְךָ יִרְבְּיֻן וְכֶסֶף וְזָהָב יִרְבֶּה לָךְ וְכֹל אֲשֶׁר לְךָ
יִרְבֶּה: וְרָם לְבָבֶךָ וְשָׁכַחְתָּ אֶת יְהוָה אֱלֹהֶיךָ הַמּוֹצִיאֲךָ מֵאֶרֶץ מִצְרַיִם מִבֵּית עֲבָדִים:
הַמּוֹלִיכֲךָ בַּמִּדְבָּר הַגָּדֹל וְהַנּוֹרָא נָחָשׁ שָׂרָף וְעַקְרָב וְצִמָּאוֹן אֲשֶׁר אֵין מָיִם הַמּוֹצִיא לְךָ
מַיִם מִצּוּר הַחַלָּמִישׁ: הַמַּאֲכִלְךָ מָן בַּמִּדְבָּר אֲשֶׁר לֹא יָדְעוּן אֲבֹתֶיךָ לְמַעַן עַנֹּתְךָ וּלְמַעַן
נַסֹּתֶךָ לְהֵיטִבְךָ בְּאַחֲרִיתֶךָ: וְאָמַרְתָּ בִּלְבָבֶךָ כֹּחִי וְעֹצֶם יָדִי עָשָׂה לִי אֶת הַחַיִל הַזֶּה: וְזָכַרְתָּ
אֶת יְהוָה אֱלֹהֶיךָ כִּי הוּא הַנֹּתֵן לְךָ כֹּחַ לַעֲשׂוֹת חָיִל לְמַעַן הָקִים אֶת בְּרִיתוֹ אֲשֶׁר נִשְׁבַּע
לַאֲבֹתֶיךָ כַּיּוֹם הַזֶּה:

יָשֵׁב רַבָּן גַּמְלִיאֵל וְדָרֵשׁ: עֲתִידָה אֶרֶץ יִשְׂרָאֵל לְהַצְמִיחַ כִּכָּרוֹת שֶׁל לֶחֶם
עַל הָעֵצִים (שַׁבָּת ל')

רַעְיוֹנוֹת

מֵהַחִטָּה עוֹשִׂים אֶת הַלֶּחֶם שֶׁהוּא עִקַּר הַמָּזוֹן שֶׁל גּוּף הָאָדָם. חִטָּה - בְּגִימַטְרִיָּה 22,
כְּנֶגֶד 22 אוֹתִיּוֹת הַתּוֹרָה שֶׁהִיא עִקַּר הַמָּזוֹן שֶׁל נִשְׁמַת הָאָדָם.

יִקְחוּ כּוֹס יַיִן אוֹ מִיץ עֲנָבִים וִיבָרְכוּ:

בָּרוּךְ אַתָּה ה' אֱלֹקֵינוּ מֶלֶךְ הָעוֹלָם בּוֹרֵא פְּרִי הַגָּפֶן:

יֹאמְרוּ פְּסוּקִים וּמִדְרָשִׁים:

וְיַיִן יְשַׂמַּח לְבַב אֱנוֹשׁ לְהַצְהִיל פָּנִים מִשָּׁמֶן וְלֶחֶם לְבַב אֱנוֹשׁ יִסְעָד:

לָמָּה הַיַּיִן נִקְרָא גַם יַיִן וְגַם תִּירוֹשׁ? יַיִן - עַל שֵׁם שֶׁמֵּבִיא יְלָלָה לָעוֹלָם, תִּירוֹשׁ - שֶׁכָּל
הַמִּתְגָּרֶה בּוֹ נַעֲשָׂה רָשׁ. רַב כַּהֲנָא רָמֵי: כְּתִיב תִּירַשׁ וְקָרֵינַן תִּירוֹשׁ, זָכָה - נַעֲשָׂה רֹאשׁ,
לֹא זָכָה - נַעֲשָׂה רָשׁ. (יוֹמָא ע"ו).

אָמַר רַבִּי שְׁמוּאֵל בַּר נַחְמָנִי אָמַר רַבִּי יוֹנָתָן: מִנַּיִן שֶׁאֵין אוֹמְרִים שִׁירָה אֶלָּא עַל הַיַּיִן?
שֶׁנֶּאֱמַר: "וַתֹּאמֶר לָהֶם הַגֶּפֶן הֶחֳדַלְתִּי אֶת תִּירוֹשִׁי הַמְשַׂמֵּחַ אֱלֹהִים וַאֲנָשִׁים" אִם
אֲנָשִׁים מְשַׂמֵּחַ - אֱלֹהִים בַּמֶּה מְשַׂמֵּחַ? מִכָּאן, שֶׁאֵין אוֹמְרִים שִׁירָה אֶלָּא עַל הַיַּיִן!
(בְּרָכוֹת לה').

ר' יְהוּדָה בֶּן בְּתֵירָה אוֹמֵר בִּזְמַן שֶׁבֵּית הַמִּקְדָּשׁ קַיָּם אֵין שִׂמְחָה אֶלָּא בְּבָשָׂר שֶׁנֶּאֱמַר:
"וְזָבַחְתָּ שְׁלָמִים וְאָכַלְתָּ שָּׁם וְשָׂמַחְתָּ לִפְנֵי ה' אֱלֹהֶיךָ" עַכְשָׁיו אֵין שִׂמְחָה אֶלָּא בְּיַיִן
שֶׁנֶּאֱמַר: וְיַיִן יְשַׂמַּח לְבַב אֱנוֹשׁ:

יִקַּח זַיִת, וְאִם אֵין לוֹ זַיִת יִקַּח תָּמָר אוֹ תְּאֵנָה אוֹ רִמּוֹן וִיבָרֵךְ בְּקוֹל רָם, וִיכַוֵּן שֶׁבְּבִרְכַּת
הָעֵץ הַזּוֹ הוּא פּוֹטֵר אֶת כָּל פֵּרוֹת הָאִילָן שֶׁיֵּשׁ עַל הַשֻּׁלְחָן.

בָּרוּךְ אַתָּה ה' אֱלֹקֵינוּ מֶלֶךְ הָעוֹלָם בּוֹרֵא פְּרִי הָעֵץ

"אֶרֶץ זָבַת חָלָב וּדְבָשׁ" - אֶרֶץ שֶׁפֵּרוֹתֶיהָ שְׁמֵנִים כְּחָלָב וּמְתוּקִים כִּדְבָשׁ!
פַּעַם אַחַת נִכְנַס רַבִּי לִבְנֵי בְרַק וּמָצָא שָׁם אֶשְׁכּוֹל עֲנָבִים מֻנָּח וְהָיָה נִרְאֶה כְּעֵגֶל בֶּן
שָׁלֹשׁ שָׁנִים:

פַּעַם אַחַת הָלַךְ רַבִּי יְהוֹשֻׁעַ לִסְכַנְיָן וּמָצָא עֵז רְבוּצָה תַּחַת עֵץ הַתְּאֵנָה וְחָלָב שׁוֹתֵת
מִמֶּנָּה וּדְבַשׁ יוֹצֵא מִן הַתְּאֵנָה וּמִתְעָרְבִּבִים זֶה בָּזֶה

לְאַחַר אֲכִילַת זַיִת יֹאמַר:

"זַיִת רַעֲנָן יְפֵה פְרִי תֹאַר קָרָא ה' שְׁמֶךָ" כְּשֵׁם שֶׁהַשֶּׁמֶן מֵאִיר - כָּךְ ביהכנ"ק מֵאִיר לְכָל הָעוֹלָם. שֶׁנֶּאֱמַר: "וְהָלְכוּ גוֹיִם לְאוֹרֵךְ", לָכֵן נִקְרְאוּ אֲבוֹתֵינוּ זַיִת רַעֲנָן שֶׁהֵם מְאִירִים לַכֹּל בֶּאֱמוּנָתָם"

לְאַחַר אֲכִילַת תָּמָר יֹאמַר:

דָּרַשׁ רַבִּי חִיָּיא בַר לוּלְיָנִי: כָּתוּב: צַדִּיק כַּתָּמָר יִפְרָח כְּאֶרֶז בַּלְּבָנוֹן יִשְׂגֶּה, אִם נֶאֱמַר תָּמָר לָמָה נֶאֱמַר אֶרֶז, וְאִם נֶאֱמַר אֶרֶז לָמָה נֶאֱמַר תָּמָר?

אִלּוּ נֶאֱמַר תָּמָר וְלֹא נֶאֱמַר אֶרֶז הָיִיתִי אוֹמֵר: מָה תָּמָר אֵין גִּזְעוֹ מַחֲלִיף - אַף צַדִּיק חַס וְחָלִילָה אֵין גִּזְעוֹ מַחֲלִיף - לְכָךְ נֶאֱמַר אֶרֶז.

אִלּוּ נֶאֱמַר אֶרֶז וְלֹא נֶאֱמַר תָּמָר, הָיִיתִי אוֹמֵר: מָה אֶרֶז אֵין עוֹשֶׂה פֵרוֹת - אַף צַדִּיק חַס וְחָלִילָה אֵין עוֹשֶׂה פֵרוֹת - לְכָךְ נֶאֱמַר תָּמָר וְנֶאֱמַר אֶרֶז (תַּעֲנִית כה')

לְאַחַר אֲכִילַת תְּאֵנָה יֹאמַר:

אָמַר רַבִּי חִיָּיא בַר אַבָּא אָמַר רַבִּי יוֹחָנָן כָּתוּב: "נוֹצֵר תְּאֵנָה יֹאכַל פִּרְיָהּ"?

לָמָה נִמְשְׁלוּ דִּבְרֵי תוֹרָה לַתְּאֵנָה? מָה עֵץ תְּאֵנָה זֶה כָּל זְמַן שֶׁאָדָם מְמַשְׁמֵשׁ בּוֹ מוֹצֵא בּוֹ תְאֵנִים. אַף דִּבְרֵי תוֹרָה כֵּן כָּל זְמַן שֶׁאָדָם הוֹגֶה בָּהֶם מוֹצֵא בָּהֶם טַעַם טוֹב.

לְאַחַר אֲכִילַת רִמּוֹן יֹאמַר:

אָמַר רֵישׁ לָקִישׁ: פּוֹשְׁעֵי יִשְׂרָאֵל אֵין אוֹר גֵּיהִנֹּם שׁוֹלֶטֶת בָּהֶן קַל וָחֹמֶר מִמִּזְבַּח הַזָּהָב, מָה מִזְבַּח הַזָּהָב שֶׁאֵין עָלָיו אֶלָּא כְעָבִי דִינָר זָהָב עָמַד כַּמָּה שָׁנִים וְלֹא שָׁלְטָה בּוֹ הָאוֹר,

פּוֹשְׁעֵי יִשְׂרָאֵל שֶׁמְּלֵיאִין מִצְווֹת כָּרִמּוֹן שֶׁנֶּאֱמַר: כְּפֶלַח הָרִמּוֹן רַקָּתֵךְ. וְאָמַר רַבִּי שִׁמְעוֹן בֶּן לָקִישׁ: אַל תִּקְרֵי רַקָּתֵךְ אֶלָּא רֵיקָתֵךְ, שֶׁאֲפִילוּ רֵיקָנִין שֶׁבָּךְ מְלֵיאִין מִצְווֹת כָּרִמּוֹן - עַל אַחַת כַּמָּה וְכַמָּה" (עֵרוּבִין דַּף יט ע"א).

לְאַחַר אֲכִילַת אֱגוֹז יֹאמַר:

אֶל גִּנַּת אֱגוֹז יָרַדְתִּי לִרְאוֹת בְּאִבֵּי הַנָּחַל לִרְאוֹת הֲפָרְחָה הַגֶּפֶן הֵנֵצוּ הָרִמֹּנִים.

לָמָה נִמְשְׁלוּ יִשְׂרָאֵל לָאֱגוֹז מָה זֶה אֱגוֹז מָה אַתָּה רוֹאֶה אוֹתוֹ כֻּלוֹ עֵץ וְאֵין תּוֹכוֹ נִכָּר, אַךְ כְּשֶׁאַתָּה פּוֹצְעוֹ אַתָּה מוֹצְאוֹ מָלֵא מְגוּרוֹת מְגוּרוֹת שֶׁל אוֹכְלִים. כָּךְ יִשְׂרָאֵל - צְנוּעִים וַעֲנָווְתָנִים בְּמַעֲשֵׂיהֶם וְאֵין תַּלְמִידִים שֶׁבָּהֶן נִכָּרִים וְאֵין מִתְפָּאֲרִים לְהַכְרִיז עַל שִׁבְחָן, אַךְ אִם אַתָּה בוֹדְקָם אַתָּה מוֹצֵא אוֹתָם מְלֵאִים חָכְמָה. וְכֵן, מָה אֱגוֹז זֶה נוֹפֵל בְּטִיט וְאֵין מַה שֶּׁבְּתוֹכוֹ נִמְאָס - אַף יִשְׂרָאֵל גּוֹלִים לְבֵין הָאֻמּוֹת וְלוֹקִים מַלְקִיּוֹת הַרְבֵּה וּבְכָל זֹאת - אֵין מַעֲשֵׂיהֶם נִמְאָסִים:

לְאַחַר אֲכִילַת אֶתְרוֹג יֹאמַר:

וּלְקַחְתֶּם לָכֶם בַּיּוֹם הָרִאשׁוֹן פְּרִי עֵץ הָדָר - זֶה הָאֶתְרוֹג. וְהוּא מְרַמֵּז עַל הַשְּׁכִינָה, וְעַל דָּוִד הַמֶּלֶךְ, וְעַל הַנְּשָׁמָה הַטְּהוֹרָה שֶׁל כָּל יְהוּדִי. וְלָכֵן צָרִיךְ לִהְיוֹת נָקִי מִכָּל פְּגָם וְכֶתֶם, כִּי הַנְּשָׁמָה טְהוֹרָה הִיא וּצְרִיכָה לְהִשָּׁאֵר נְקִיָּה מֵחֶטְאֵי הָעוֹלָם.

לְאַחַר אֲכִילַת תַּפּוּחַ יֹאמַר:

כְּתַפּוּחַ בַּעֲצֵי הַיַּעַר כֵּן דּוֹדִי בֵּין הַבָּנִים בְּצִלּוֹ חִמַּדְתִּי וְיָשַׁבְתִּי וּפִרְיוֹ מָתוֹק לְחִכִּי:

לָמָה נִמְשַׁל הַקָּבָּ"ה לְתַפּוּחַ? לוֹמַר לְךָ מָה תַּפּוּחַ זֶה נִרְאָה לָעַיִן בְּלֹא כְלוּם אַךְ בֶּאֱמֶת יֵשׁ בּוֹ טַעַם וְרֵיחַ, כָּךְ הַקָּבָּ"ה חִכּוֹ מַמְתַּקִּים וְכֻלּוֹ מַחֲמַדִּים וְנִרְאָה לְעוֹבְדֵי כּוֹכָבִים וְלֹא רָצוּ לְקַבֵּל הַתּוֹרָה, וְהָיְתָה הַתּוֹרָה בְּעֵינֵיהֶם כְּדָבָר שֶׁאֵין בּוֹ מַמָּשׁ, וּבֶאֱמֶת יֵשׁ בּוֹ טַעַם וְרֵיחַ, טַעַם כִּמְנַיִן? שֶׁנֶּאֱמַר (תְּהִלִּים לד) טַעֲמוּ וּרְאוּ כִּי טוֹב ה', וְיֵשׁ בּוֹ מַאֲכָל דִּכְתִיב (מִשְׁלֵי ח) טוֹב פִּרְיִי מֵחָרוּץ וּמִפָּז, וְיֵשׁ בּוֹ רֵיחַ שֶׁנֶּאֱמַר (שִׁיר הַשִּׁירִים ד) וְרֵיחַ שַׂלְמֹתַיִךְ כְּרֵיחַ לְבָנוֹן, אָמְרוּ יִשְׂרָאֵל אָנוּ יוֹדְעִין כֹּחָהּ שֶׁל תּוֹרָה לְפִיכָךְ אֵין אָנוּ זָזִים מִן הַקָּבָּ"ה וְתוֹרָתוֹ, שֶׁנֶּאֱמַר: בְּצִלּוֹ חִמַּדְתִּי וְיָשַׁבְתִּי וּפִרְיוֹ מָתוֹק לְחִכִּי.

יִקְחוּ פְּרִי מִפֵּרוֹת הָאֲדָמָה וִיבָרְכוּ:

בָּרוּךְ אַתָּה ה' אֱלֹקֵינוּ מֶלֶךְ הָעוֹלָם בּוֹרֵא פְּרִי הָאֲדָמָה

יִקְחוּ מַשְׁקֶה כָּלְשֶׁהוּ וִיבָרְכוּ:

בָּרוּךְ אַתָּה ה' אֱלֹקֵינוּ מֶלֶךְ הָעוֹלָם שֶׁהַכֹּל נִהְיָה בִּדְבָרוֹ

שִׁירִים הַקְּשׁוּרִים לְטוּ בִּשְׁבָט:

צַדִּיק כַּתָּמָר יִפְרָח, אֶרֶץ חִטָּה וּשְׂעוֹרָה, אֶרֶץ זָבַת חָלָב, עֵץ חַיִּים הִיא, וְהָיָה כְּעֵץ שָׁתוּל, בָּרְכֵנוּ ה' אֱלֹקֵינוּ, אֶרֶץ אֲשֶׁר תָּמִיד.

בְּרָכָה אַחֲרוֹנָה לְאַחַר שְׁתִיַּת רְבִיעִית מַשְׁקֶה אוֹ אַחַר פֵּרוֹת שֶׁאֵינָם מִשִּׁבְעַת הַמִּינִים

בָּרוּךְ אַתָּה ה', אֱלֹהֵינוּ מֶלֶךְ הָעוֹלָם, בּוֹרֵא נְפָשׁוֹת רַבּוֹת, וְחֶסְרוֹנָן עַל כָּל מַה שֶּׁבָּרָאתָ לְהַחֲיוֹת בָּהֶם נֶפֶשׁ כָּל חַי בָּרוּךְ חַי הָעוֹלָמִים.

TU B'AV

TU B'AV

Prelude to Yom Kippur

According to early Talmudic scholars, Tu b'Av (the 15th day of the month of Av) was at one time a very important holiday. It has within it of the essence of forgiveness of sins which is found on Yom Kippur.

This holiday, due to its holy and pure nature, often served as the date on which young couples began their engagement period, for it was thought that under the auspices of this reverent occasion, the chastity and modesty of Israel would not be in danger of being breached.

The quality of forgiveness inherent in this day manifested itself fully in relation to the generation in the desert.

The spies committed their grievous sin on the 9th of Av. Every year from then on fifteen thousand men died on that date. On the last year, when the people saw that the full moon, the 15th of Av, had arrived and none had died, they realized that they had been forgiven, and they rejoiced.

Their great joy caused God's speaking to Moses which had been somewhat curtailed since the sin to return to its former clarity.

This happiness of Israel over their pardon, and the subsequent clarity of God's speech to Moses, instilled in this day an everlasting affinity for purity and revelation of holiness. Only with the destruction of the Temple did this great happiness subside.

The precious quality of this day also revealed itself in a later period, as pointed out by our honored sages in the Gemara tractate *Ta'anith*. There we are told that it had been a practice at one time to limit intermarriage between the members of the different tribes of Israel in order to preserve the inheritance within a tribe.

However, it was decided during the period of the judges to repeal this enactment because the great scholars of that era had discovered from the words of the Torah that the limitations for intermarriage between the tribes were only relevant to the generation that conquered the land. This new ruling took place on the 15th of Av.

Another, similar ruling took place on this date: When the tribe of Benjamin committed the loathsome act against the concubine in *Giv'ah* (Judges 19), the other tribes vowed not to intermarry with Benjamin; on the 15th of Av, it was determined that this vow pertained only to that specific generation.

The very date, the 15th of Av, indicates the appropriateness of these occurrences on this day. 15 is the equivalent of the first two letters of God's name.

These two letters are also the two letters in the Hebrew words for man (איש) and woman (אשה) that are not the same, signifying the third link in the male-female relationship.

The above-mentioned events crowned the 15th of Av with positive spiritual influences which were to continue throughout history.

PURIM

PURIM

PURIM CONTAINS ALL FESTIVALS

Purim is the holiday that ends all the holidays of the year. It is a holiday that stores within it the virtues of all the holy days in the cycle of the year. This is implied in the initial letters - ‏פסח‎- Pesach and—‏וסוכות‎Succoth- ‏ראש‎ -‏השנה‎ Rosh Hashanah, ‏כפור‎- ‏יום‎ Yom Kippur-Day of atonement.

On Purim, things that happened are similar to those that happened in the Festivals of the year. Deliverance from slavery to freedom, in Purim, as in Passover. Purim is a festival, of unity and peace, like the holiday of Sukkoth, Rosh Hashanah, and the Day of Judgment as Purim is when Jews face judgment in heaven on whether to live or die by the decree of the evil Haman.

Fasting and praying in Purim like Yom Kippur, Day of Atonement. Purim is when Jews faced judgment in heaven on whether to live or die by the decree of the evil Haman, as on Rosh Hashanah, the Day of Judgment. Fasting and praying in Purim like Yom Kippur, the Day of Atonement.

PURIM AND SUCCOTH

The Book of Heritage brings another reason for the similarity of Sukkoth to Purim, just as Sukkoth commemorate the protection accorded us by the divine cloud of glory in the wilderness, likewise did many non-Jews enter under the protecting of divinity during Purim by converting to Judaism.

The Acceptance of the Torah out of love on Purim, as is written in the Book of Esther, "was observed and accepted by the Jews", as in giving the Torah on Shavuot, on Purim Jews repented out of love when they realized the great miracles that GOD did for them.

The power of repentance in Purim is indicated in the full numerical value of the letters פורים - -Purim, פי, ואו,ריש,יוד,מם 713=90+13+510+20+80))the same numerical value of the word תשובה- repentance(,400+300+6+2+5=713).

THE ESSENCE OF THE NAME PURIM

The essence of the name פורים -Purim lies in the letters - פר PR which signify might and strength as the letterפ -P and - ר R, represent, as can be heard in their pronunciation as in many words which have these letters, as the word power, etc. as I brought in my "Hebrew source of languages".

Words which start with פר - PR, פר-ד, פרד -separate, פרץ -breaking through פרק -taking apart. In his words of Haman to Achashverosh against Jews in Persia, he said, there is a nation in your kingdom מפרד - separated, not united people, and it is worthwhile exterminating them.

MEANING OF THE NAME רפידים REFIDIM

Interesting to note what our commentator Kli Yakar say about the place רפידים -Refidim, the place the Amalek attacked Jews in the desert, the letter פרידים are the same letters as the word פרידים -separated, indicating it that because of no unity among Jews Amalek came to attack them.

Another interpretation of the name רפידים according to our Rabbis, is the words—רפ-ידים -loose hands indicating that because Jews were loose-handed in fulfilling the Torah Amalek came to attack them.

Both reasons given for the name רפידים complement each other, as disunity among Jews brings Amalek to fight with them. This is what was the situation in פורים -Purim, indicating in the numerical value of the word 356)ברפידים) the same numerical value as (356)פורים Purim.

Those traits in a negative way were embodied by the wicked Haman and his counselors. Purim is the holiday that ends all the holidays of the year. It is a holiday that stores within it the virtues of all the good holidays in the cycle of the year.

This is implied in the initials letters –פורים-Purim—פסח Pesach and -וסוכותSukkoth- ראש השנה- -Rosh Hashanah-יום כפור- Yom Kipur-מתן תורה giving the Torah, as we saw before.

On Purim, things that happened were similar to those that happened in the Festivals of the year. Deliverance from slavery to freedom, in Purim, as in Passover.

Purim is a festival, of unity and peace, like the holiday of Sukkoth, Rosh Hashanah, Judgment Day, Purim when Jews face judgment in heaven on whether to live or die by the decree of the evil Haman, as on Rosh Hashanah, the day of Judgment. Fasting and praying in Purim like Yom Kippur, the Day of Atonement.

The Acceptance of the Torah out of love on Purim, as is written in the Book of Esther, "was observed and accepted by the Jews", as in giving the Torah on Shavuot.

THE ESSENCE OF THE NAME פורים PURIM

The essence of the name פורים - Purim lies in the letters פר -PR which signify might and harsh judgment which came out and threatened the existence of the people of Israel. Israel's' wholehearted repentance like on Yom Kippur, the Day of transformed them into holiness. Atonement, humbled these hash judgment and evil forces into submission and

This spiritual triumph spurred the Jews to victory over their enemies in the temporal world. The letter VAV , according to the Zohar is the letter of holiness, interceded between the letter פר - PR, the letters of might and strength, and turned them into the letters - which are the letters, which are the source of the word פורים - PURIM as we will see -פור PUR latter.

The book *Bnei Yissaschar* states that the letter VAV , ו is also the letter of life, so when joined to the letters פר- PR and the word פור - **Pur** comes out. It indicates the salvation of Israel from death, and their assurance of continued life even in the world to come, similar to the holiday of Passover.

LETTER ו ACCORDING TO KABBALAH

The letter VAV– ו according the Zohar is the letter of knowledge and truth, by Jews getting the knowledge and the truth of the Torah , they manage to separate the letters of power פר - PR and change it to פור – PUR, the source of פורים- –Purim. The letterer VAV ו , represents unity, it was the unity of Jews that annulled the strength of the letters פר- PR.

The letter VAV its, numerical value is six, indicating to the six sets of Mishnah, the source of the Oral Torah, that Jew accepted upon them on Purim. Six is the number of the sphere יסוד – Foundation, the sphere representing purity.

.

THE MEANING OF THE LETTER ו VAV

The letter VAV ,ורepresent also שלום- peace , Peace which connected with Purim is indicated in the inner numerical value of the full letters of מם פורים פי,וו,ריש,יוד, inner letters are 376 376=10+6+310+10+40),(י',ו,יש,ד,ום) the same numerical value of the word 376=300+30+6+40) שלום). Interesting to note that the scroll of Ester is called (9;30) " words of peace and truth".

Purim 80+6+200+10 +40=336) (336) (פורים-) has the same numerical value as the words -המןHaman (95) (5+40+50=95) and עמלק-Amalek (240) (70+40+30+100=240) with the total 336,(95+240=335).

The numerical value of Purim-336, ONE more then המן עמלק-Haman Amalek -335 shows the power of Purim with the help of ONE GOD to fight against the evil forces, of Hama and Amalek.

The number 336 is the same numerical value as the word בפורים - In Purim, which is the same numerical value of the evil heavenly angles רהב- –Rav ((207and סמאל –Samael (131)(207+131=338). Evil forces have to do with Edom and Ishmael, Lust and Pride.

Against these evil forces stand יעקב – -Jacob (182) and his son יוסף – Joseph (156) (182 +156=338) will fight these two evil forces, as stated (in Obad. 18):

"THE HOUSE OF JACOB SHALL BE A FIRE, AND THE USE OF JOSEPH A FLAME AND THE HOUSE OF ESAU SHALL BE STRAW";

The number 336 is six times the number 56 which is the numerical value of the word יום- Day (10+6+40=56) Purim 336 brings the book Kehilat Yakov,(a Key to the doctrine of the Kabala) has in it the essence of the six days, which correspond to the six spheres.

Ben Ish chai says that the number 336 is the numerical value of three times the name of GOD representing the attribute of Judgment, the name, 86) א-להים)and three times the name of GOD which represents Mercy 26) י-ה-ו-ה) , indicating to the situation of Jews in Purim, similar idea of the letters פ-ר- P-R which change to פור- PUR. Interesting to note that the numerical value of the word 78 -מגלה scroll (40+3+30+5=78 is three times the name of GOD of Mercy -26)(26)ה-ו-ה-יX3=78).

SIGN OF THE ZODIAC OF THE MONTH ADAR

This change of Jews in Purim is indicated in the zodiac of the month אדר- Adar, the דג -the Fish, the letter דלת,ד representing דלות

–poverty, while the letter גימל ,ג, representing granting and giving, by a rich man, what Jew got in the end.

The situation of the Jews in Persia as poor and miserable is indicated in the name of the month אדר the letter ד and the letter ר represent poverty דל –רש, meaning a poor man. The letter א in the word אדר א,אלף, represents GOD who saved them from this situation.

On Purim, says Rav Nachman of Breslau, the hidden light is shining like on the Sabbath, this can be seen from the full numerical value of the letters of the word ור,ריש,יוד,מם,(703=81+12+510+20+80)פורים פא,. The number 703 is the numerical value of)(703) the wordשבת Sabbath with the total,(300+2+400+1=703).

Our sacred books learn from that on Purim there are powers prevalent that can wipe out the evil for which Haman and Amalek stand. The equivalent numerical value also symbolizes the struggle if the forces of good against the forces of evil.

MESSIAH -358 -SNAKE -358

Another example of this case is the equivalent numerical value of the words משיח- Messiah (40+300+10+8=358) and נחש- Snake (50+8+300=358). In this scheme, the snake represents the root of Amalek. The identical numerical values teach us that the Messiah will incapacitate the primeval snake, the source of evil in the world.

Purim is a time when the material forces which are the weapon wielded by the Satan in his war with holiness are brought to submission by holiness and even turned back against the Satan. For this reason, the commandments of Purim revolve around eating and drinking. Amalek the descendant of Esau is the source of strife and division in the world.

AMALEK THE EVIL FORCE OF THE SATAN

עמלק -Amalek is the evil force of the Satan, the evil inclination in man, who brings into man's mind and heart doubts in the belief in GOD. Idea which is indicated in the numerical value of the word 240) (ספק) –Doubt (60+80+100=240), which is the same numerical value of the word –Amalek-70+40+30+100) (עמלק).

It is interesting to note that the numerical value of these two words numerical value-(240,+240=480) becomes 480, which is the numerical value of the evil angle Lilith-30+10+30+10+40) (480) (לילית 0)

These traits of argumentativeness and hatred, Amalek inherited from his grandfather Esau. Esau עשו- has the same numerical value as the שלום- Shalom– Peace informs us, according to our learned Rabbis, that Esau represents the complete opposite of peace, and that if Esau is eliminated from the world peace will come.

There is another interpretation as to why Purim is derived from the word פור -PUR (lottery). The Bnei Yissaschar informs us that the name Purim is intended to show Israel the great loving-kindness with which GOD has treated them. GOD ordained that פור (lottery) Haman intended to destroy the Jews, would fall during the month of Adar, a month which historically has always proved to be very auspicious for Israel.

THE MEANING OF THE NAME אדר ADAR

The meaning of the word אדר -Adar comes from the term אדיר - Adir, denoting strength. It is a month which, due to its quality and importance is the scheme of creation, is more suitable for Israel redemption and salvation than any other month.

A clear manifest indication of Israel's redemption and salvation was not given to the holiday Purim, since the salvation associated with the holiday occurred by means of subtle miracles, shrouded by the course of natural events.

The miracles only surface when one reads carefully from the scroll of Esther are that which -מגלה the scroll of Esther, מגלה - reveals the הסתר -hidden mysteries of the days of Purim.

This latency of GOD's miracles is hinted by the verse in the scriptures which states" ...and I will surely hide my face from that on that day". אסתר - Esther the queen was appointed by Heaven to bring to the fore GODS's obscured countenance. The name אסתר - א, אלף-סתר -indicates the fact that אלוף –GOD was hidden.

Purim is the beginning of the preparation for Passover, a preparation for total redemption. An added dimension to this preparation for the Sabbath on which the portion about the -פרה אדמה the Red Heifer.

According to Kabala the portion of the פרה –Heifer which is read from the Torah on the Sabbath, changes the attribute of hash Judgment by the letter ה like the letter VAV ו, change the -פר PR into -פור PUR the source of Purim.

PURIM AND KIPURIM

This similarity is seen in the words פורים and כפורים, the word כפורים is like (כ) Purim, showing that פורים Purim is greater the *Kippurim*. Interesting explanation for it brings the book of heritage. "On Yom Kippur Jews ascend to a level whereby they transcend the constraints of nature by denying themselves physical satisfaction and thus achieve atonement for the sins of the body.

On Purim, the same level of holiness is achieved through eating and drinking so the physical pleasures become imbued with holiness".

This idea comes from our previous explanation of the letters-פר PR representing the powers of the physical. On Yom Kippur יום כפור, whose root is the word כפר (כ)כף פר we force the פר -PR, the powers of nature, while on Purim we sanctify them and elevate them to a very high level.

THE LETTERS פר PR

The letters פר –PR represent strong powers which is seen in the numerical value of the letters 280=80+200)280 - פר) a number which is ten times the word strength -28=20+8) כח).

As we saw before, the scroll of Esther is called "–"דברי אמת ושלום" words of Peace and Truth", as the truth of the divine providence of GOD, came out clearly to the whole world, as the Sage says the verse in Isaiah (52:10)

"'The LORD will bare His holy arm in the sight of all the nations, And the very ends of the earth shall see The victory of our God", which refers to the story of Purim.

פורים - Purim brought peace to Jews and strengthened their unity as the commandants of Purim show, sending of portions one to the other, presents to the poor, etc. These attributes Jews got by מרדכי ואסתר— Mordechai and Esther.

An interesting indication to this in the numerical value of מרדכי and אסתר which with the total have the same numerical value as the word שלום- peace שלום- ((936) (936= 1+ 661+ 274- מרדכי -אסתר– peace, when the final letter ם , has the numerical value of 600 (300+30+6+600=936).

MEANING OF THE NAME מרדכי -MORDECHAI

Interesting meaning to the names- מרדכי Mordechai and- אסתר Esther. The name מרדכי contains two words דכי, מר, מר means bitter, the numerical value of the word מר, is 240 (40+200=240) the same numerical value of the name -עמלק –Amelek, as we saw before.

The word דכי means crushing. Indicating that מרדכי goal was to destroy Amalek (240). Our sage tells us that Mordechai was like Moses in his doings for the Jewish people in Persia. Our Rabbi say that the name מרדכי is the name of one of the spices which was in the incent and has a good smell.

The myrtle with the good smell in the lulav taken on the festival of Succoth indicates to people with good deeds. Similarly is Esther who had another name, הדסה , connected with the myrtle which gives a good smell.

This fact is indicated in the numerical value of his title in the scroll of Esther 311+35=346) איש יהודי) a man from Judah (connected to the tribe of יהודה -Judah, (from his mother side), as the numerical value of משה –Moses, with the total (40+300+5+1=346).

Another explanation to the title מרדכי היהודי -Mordechai the Jew- יהודי, is as the word יחודי -Only One, indicating that Mordechai believed in GOD who is אחד – One. According to Rabbi Isaac Luria. Mordechai was the incarnation of Jacob, while Haman was the incarnation of Esau.

Yaakov and Mordechai

An interesting idea comes from the numerical value of the names מרדכי and (יעקב) 456=182+274) which is the same numerical as the prohibition to serve idles, as it is written in the Torah "לא יהיה לך (אלהים אחרים)" 456=31+30+50+86+259) You should not have other gods".

Another kabbalistic source says that Jacob was the incarnation of Adam, and Esther was the Incarnation of חוה -Eve, so that Mordeachai and Esther were basically Adam and Eve.

Adam and Eve by sinning by eating from the tree of knowledge brought troubles to the Jews, and their mission over History is to rectify ii.

The purpose of the commandments of Purim is the rectification of the sin, of eating from the עץ הדעת - the Tree of Knowledge. The Rectification which started from TU B'shvat, by eating the fruits.

MEANING OF THE NAME אסתר - ESTHER

The name -אסתר Esther contains two parts א, -סתר, the letter א, אלף, represents GOD who is אלוף של עולם - the Aloof of the world, and the word סתר – meaning hidden. As Esther showed that GOD is also functioning when it looked like he was hidden. Her name אסתר indicates also to the fact that Esther kept secretes, as she did not reveal that she is Jewish

אסתר has another name -שושנה –**rose,** as we sing after reading the Megilah שושנת יעקב -The Rose of Jacob. Our Rabbis say that Esther got this name שושנה because אסתר שינתה –changed, the situation of the Jews in Persia by bringing them to repentance which saved their life.

ANOTHER NAME OF ESTHER

The connection between the name אסתר and the name שושנה is seen from the same numerical value, 661.אסתר 661=300+6+300+50+5 שושנה,(661=1+60+400+200)). The number 661 indicates in its numbers to the thirteen attributes of the Mercy of GOD(1+6+6=13) .

Thirteen is the numerical value of the word 13=8+1+4-) אחד אחד) –One. Interestingly, the minor numerical value of the names of מרדכי and אסתר are thirteen.(13=1+6+4+2) אסתר, and the name מרדכי 13=4+2+4+2+1)).Their names show that they brought unity to the Jewish people in Persia 'which saved them.

Interesting to note that 13 +13=26,26 is the numerical value of the name of GOD, the name representing the attribute of Mercy י-ה-ו-ה, which אסתר and מרדכי revealed.

Interesting to note that the number of verses in the scroll of Esther 166, the same number of words in the Torah about Amalek, the story that we read in the Torah on Sabbath Zachor, and on Purim.

It is known that in the story of Scroll of Esther, there are indications of the mascaras of Jews in the years 5408-9 -1648 and in the holocaust in Germany.

The indication to it is in the enlarged letter ת in the word ותכתב, and in the enlarged letter ח in the word חור. The numerical value of the letter ת is four hundred, and the numerical value of the letter ח is eight, together 408, indicating to this year.

BIG AND THE SMALL LETTERS IN THE MEGILAH

The small letters are in the names of Haman's sons. The letters תשז, whose numerical value is 707. Interestingly, the number 7 in this number is the number of the seventh sphere מלכות – kingdom.

The number 700 hundred represents the sphere of the kingdom in the high world, the world of creation. The number 7 represents this world of action, the lower world. The letters תשז have the numerical value 707, the year after the end of the second world war. .

The interesting idea brings Rabbi Glatstein in his book "The Concealed and the Revealed ", about the small letters in the name of the children of Haman in the Megilah. He says that the letters - – תשז 707- indicating to the year 5707 -1947, are small because in this year Amalek was reduced as their might was diminished with the execution of the ten criminals.

According to the book *Manos Aharonthe* ten Nazi criminals, who were hanged were the reincarnations of the sons of Haman who were executed. He says that Hitler was the reincarnation of Haman, indicating to the defeat of Amalek.

It is interesting to note that the numerical value of the name היטלר -Hitler with the total is (245) (1+5+9+30+200=245) as the numerical value of the name עמלק , The Amalek (100+30+40+70+5=245).

The decreasing number 7, from 700 to 7, in the number of 707, as we explained before, might indicate the diminishing of Amalek might, which before was very strong, and in the year 707 in the sixth millennia (which is indicated in the big latter וin the name ויזתא , the letter ו whose numerical value is six) diminished.

The idea is based on the words of Achashveirosh to Esther that a decree which was sealed by the king cannot be abolished, so the decree to exterminate and to kill the Jewish people was postponed to latter generations.

As is known where the name מלך -King in the megilah mentioned without the name Achashverus it refers to GOD.

Interesting fact that for the redeemers of Israel from the time of משה and אהרן , the first letters of their names are the same, the letter א and אהרן – משה .מ in Egypt, אסתר –מרדכי in Persia אליהו –משיח in the future redemption.

The two leaders in Israel represent the Intellectual, the brain, and the emotional, the heart.

Moses who gave the Torah the laws of GOD, to the children of Israel, represents the mind, while Aaron the priest was in charge of the service of GOD by offerings and prayers, represents the heart

Mordechai who according to Kabala was a spark of Moses, taught the children of Israel the Torah of GOD which they accepted then willingly, after they accepted it under force in Sinai. While Esther the queen instilled into the heart of the children of Israel the faith of GOD.

Similarly משיח - Messiah and אליהו –Elijah. Elijah, about whom the prophet Malachi (4:6) says, "He will turn the hearts of the parents to their children, and the hearts of the children to their parents;"

While Messiah says the prophet Habakkuk (2:14) "For the earth will be filled with the knowledge of the glory of the LORD as the waters cover the sea".

As in the positive leaders, there are two against the heart and against the mind, so there are, also in the negative, one who represents the brain the intellectual, and one who represents the heart. Those were King Achashveiros and Haman. Haman who with his intellect gave to King Achashveiros reasons why to exterminate the Jewish people, so that King Achshveiros hatred in his heart against Jews will be strong, and he will agree to bring out the decree, to exterminate the Jews.